# THE BOOK COFFEE
## A Philosophy

# THE BOOK COFFEE
## A Philosophy

Julian Baggini
*with James Hoffmann*

MITCHELL BEAZLEY

# CONTENTS

| | | |
|---|---|---|
| | Foreword | 7 |
| i | A Cup of Humanity | 23 |
| ii | Tao and Zen | 43 |
| iii | Flowers | 73 |
| iv | The Café | 89 |
| v | The Schools of Coffee | 107 |
| vi | Aesthetic Appreciation | 125 |
| vii | Coffee Masters | 141 |
| | Afterword | 151 |
| | Index | 170 |
| | About the Authors | 174 |

# Foreword

'It's just coffee!'

If you're someone like me, someone who takes great pleasure in coffee, then you've probably heard this phrase dozens of times – often spoken in exasperation as a response to an explanation about why we might find coffee so engrossing and delightful. It was not, I confess, a phrase I have had a particularly good relationship with until the manuscript for this book arrived.

The manuscript came through a friend; there was little explanation of the contents, and my brain did not make the connection to the classic of culture, philosophy and ritual that is *The Book of Tea*. Therefore, when I read the title, I feared the worst: a little book of coffee trivia to be sold cheaply in shops that aren't really bookshops. I certainly did not expect something as philosophically transformational as the present book would turn out to be. I read it for the first time in a single sitting, slightly confused that a topic that I was so familiar with could be used to draw out fresh insights and ideas.

I spend a lot of my life thinking about the relationship people have with coffee, both as individuals and as a culture. This drink has spread to be a truly global thing, intertwining itself into every culture in every country on the planet. We really do like coffee a lot, and it is more than a dependency. If it was, truly, just about the caffeine, there are cheaper and more effective ways to get it. Caffeine is readily available in pill form, but we'd much rather have the inconvenience of the drink because of how it makes us feel. I'm not denying that caffeine isn't a large part of why we drink coffee daily, but I think it is a smaller piece than we sometimes give it credit for.

Our relationship with coffee has changed greatly over the last twenty years, particularly in the last five. Speciality coffee

Caffeine is readily available
in pill form, but we'd much rather
have the inconvenience of the drink
because of how it makes us feel.

arrived, blossoming worldwide, and suddenly coffee tasted more interesting, had many more stories about where it had come from, and went from the fringes of café culture to being widely available. First into every city, then into every town, came independent coffee shops as well as multinational chains masquerading as independent coffee shops. Coffee had long been seen as a cheap necessity. It was the famous example of a 'loss leader' in supermarkets; a product sold so cheaply that they lost money on it, in order to bring customers in for their weekly shop. Even as a drink, we had long expected it to be cheap. We all remember the bitter brutality of the complimentary coffee of hotels, conferences and places we gathered. Yet this new, more expensive form of coffee quickly won people over.

A friend of mine who works in craft chocolate argues that one of the reasons coffee was so successful was that it was an easy upgrade: you were going to get a latte anyway, so why not get one that tastes much nicer for a relatively small premium? Swapping out the everyday for the speciality version was often described as a little luxury, a phrase I didn't particularly mind until the apparent excess and indulgence of a tasty cup of coffee and a plate of avocado toast became the dismissive reason the tabloid newspapers offered for why a generation couldn't afford to get on the housing ladder. There had long been jokes that the kind of coffee you drink gives something away about the kind of person you are, but the kind of coffee shop you went to also became a kind of self-expression. We liked a lot about how drinking better coffee made us feel, aside from the occasional interaction with the unpleasant cliché of the coffee snob.

From the early 2000s onward, speciality coffee grew steadily, seemingly immune to shifting economies and proving more durable than a fad or trend. Delicious coffee had worked its way into many of our lives when the COVID-19 pandemic hit, and suddenly it was taken away from us. Cafés closed, societies were placed into various levels of lockdown, and many of us who worked in coffee worried that this would cause an irrevocable collapse in our industry. Those worries did not last long.

Almost immediately, there was a scramble in most countries and cultures to bring coffee into people's homes, so they needn't give up this little luxury, this simple nicety that they had grown so accustomed to. I don't think any of us in the coffee industry anticipated that by bringing coffee into our homes, we'd develop an entirely new relationship with it. For many of us, this brought a new ritual into our homes, at a time when rituals turned out to have unexpected value. Stuck at home, we found time suddenly stretchy and unpleasantly elastic, and so many of us found real, meaningful value in stepping away from work to spend some time on something simple but rewarding.

I looked forward to my second cup of the day, not the one that fired up the cognitive engine but the one that allowed a pause.

The act of brewing coffee became, for millions of people, a highlight of their day. We looked forward to it, revelled in it and enjoyed the lingering pleasure that coffee offered us. Buoyed by a moment of pleasure, invigorated by both the psychoactive compounds and the little investment in the self, we were able to continue with our day. I remember quite clearly how much I looked forward to my second cup of the day, not the one that fired up the cognitive engine but the one that allowed a pause. I remember a feeling of liberation as I stepped away from the laptop, the portal to both the responsibilities of work and also the swirling maelstrom of the internet – a place full of fear, confusion, anger and anxiety. To leave that behind, to spend some time in the kitchen going through a sequence of weighing and grinding and brewing, was already something I enjoyed, but the contrast to everything else made it an even deeper pleasure. Even if the resulting cup had to come back with me to my desk, I had found some space for a different kind of thought, and that was meaningful.

The ritual of coffee making developed a new power for many, and as reluctant as I am to describe it as a spiritual moment, it is hard to argue that there wasn't something nourishing about it for many of us. For me, this was the moment that coffee reached a kind of parity with tea.

For centuries, some cultures have enjoyed the wider ritual of tea and have leveraged it into an experience with more meaning than just a gustatory one. The taste of the tea was important, of course, forming a key part of the aesthetic experience, but it was only a piece of the puzzle. The particular rituals coffee has developed are rooted in flavour, or they are perhaps now more focused than our previous coffee rituals on achieving a taste that is at least delicious, and which, at its best, offers a kind of true 'taste of place' (I'm loath to steal the term *terroir* from the world of wine!).

The new culture of coffee is centred around an idea of a taste of place, that everything should be as transparent as possible in the process – from harvesting to roasting to brewing – and how we brew coffee is built around that idea. To brew a cup with less acidity might, for some, make a cup that is preferable but one that is perhaps less true to the inherent acidity that comes from the coffee itself, and so for a time the less acidic cup was considered inferior. While that hasn't really changed, I think more people also enjoy brewing coffee for the opportunity it brings to perform a ritual, and this book is a great exploration of that theme, one that will only deepen that enjoyment.

Coincidentally, I first read this book during a strange moment of crisis. Or, perhaps more precisely, this book caused lingering and disparate feelings to merge into a feeling of discomfort. Coffee is the fuel of productivity, and it has been this way for hundreds of years. In the mid-1600s, coffee arrived in London and produced a surprising cultural upheaval. The English had been a nation drinking a great deal of weak beer every day, a drink that was safe and offered some nutrition of sorts. Coffee became an alternative, and with it came the effect of caffeine on culture. London's coffeehouses became the driver of culture and business. The most famous example is Lloyd's Coffee House, which developed a reputation as a place to discuss insurance for sailing vessels. This slowly morphed into the powerhouse of Lloyd's of London, the insurer in an iconic building where the runners are still referred to as waiters. Later, another culture would take up coffee as a champion of work and productivity. When the United States of America threw a bunch of tea into Boston Harbor, rejecting both Britain and its taxation demands, it made coffee a most American drink. Coffee became the fuel of hustle culture, of the American Dream.

While it might have been our break from work during the pandemic, caffeine was also the drug we turned to in order to keep productivity high. It feeds early morning starts and carries us through late-night sessions. Many have subscribed to the idea of 'death before decaf' because to them the real utility of coffee is in – and please know I truly hate this pun – the grind.

Productivity is a word I have a very difficult relationship with. It is often how we measure ourselves, measure our time in jobs or even our time in this life. But at the root of it is something I like, a question that I find useful: what did I make or create or do today? I think it is no bad thing to think about whether you used your time well, or how you might want to make or do more today than you did yesterday. My growing discomfort with the word came from the realisation that we speak about productivity through the lens of individualism. Everywhere, there are people asking, 'How can I be more productive?', but we don't exist in isolation. Reading *The Book of Coffee* made me think about collectivism again and wonder, 'How do *we* do more?'

What is so appealing about the ideas in this book is that we could pivot this drink from being the driving force behind excessive hours and a poor work-life balance into being a drink that lets us contemplate meaning and purpose in a different way. The tea ceremony's power and meaning put it behind a barrier. Tea ceremonies are, for many Western readers, most likely to be enjoyed only as tourists, with participation only skin deep and nuance and meaning hidden behind the alien and the foreign to those of us who have limited understanding and experience of thoughtful tea brewing. Most of us don't realise that our experience with brewing coffee at home, this simple ritual born

We could pivot this drink from being the driving force behind a poor work–life balance into being a drink that lets us contemplate meaning and purpose in a different way.

from the strangest place, has deepened our understanding of a process to the point that we can enjoy it philosophically as well as enjoying the resulting drink and the little lift of caffeine, too. Coffee's ephemeral nature extends to the places we drink it. The London boom in speciality coffee is over twenty years old, and in that time we've already seen things shift and change. My own relationship with the city I live in is deeply connected to coffee shops, but not because I've worked in the coffee industry for that long. A coffee shop was the first place that gave me a sense of belonging in a city that I'd lived in for nearly a decade. As I sat in the small but excellent coffee shop near my flat that was named for an obscure song by Gladys Knight & the Pips, it seemed inevitable that I'd bump into someone I knew, or would have a quick chat with an increasingly familiar face. This made me feel connected with the people who lived around me – a feeling I'd not felt before. London had been a lonely, disconnected and isolating place.

That coffee shop is now closed. I genuinely mourned its loss, and I don't think I've found anywhere that truly replaces it. In that sadness is a tremendous beauty for which I'm incredibly grateful. Not many people get that feeling, not in places like London. That might be the pastoral ideal of the village pub, but anonymity always felt like the currency of cities. I love that coffee offers that opportunity, and that something as simple as having a shared interest in a great cup of coffee, or a shared appreciation of a vibe or aesthetic, is enough to bind people together.

As you prepare to turn the page and start the book proper, you might still be sceptical. I've promised that this book will offer you far more from a cup of coffee. Even if you have fallen in love with the diverse flavours of coffee and its complexities, even if you've used it to explore continents or have rejected caffeine due to the discovery that decaf can be wonderful, you may still be wondering how this drink could be a pathway to discuss philosophy and the very meaning of life.

After all, it's just coffee. Isn't it?

—James Hoffmann

When we consider how small after all the cup of human enjoyment is, how soon overflowed with tears, how easily drained to the dregs in our quenchless thirst for infinity, we shall not blame ourselves for making so much of the tea-cup.

—Kakuzō Okakura, *The Book of Tea* (1906)

# i
# A Cup of Humanity

The first time I encountered the wisest book I have ever read, I returned it unread to the shelf of a Tokyo bookshop and left. *The Book of Tea* by Kakuzō Okakura (1863–1913) had caught my eye but I did not trust my own judgement. Was it a genuine classic of Japanese thought, as the jacket claimed, or an outdated curio, written in 1906 for Westerners with an eye for the romantic and the exotic and still appealing to travellers and tourists today?

The answer was both and neither. Even when it was written, the book was a kind of elegy-in-waiting for a tradition that was already being lost. Today, there are Japanese who have never partaken in a tea ceremony, while for the rest it is a rare occurrence. Okakura's paean to what he called 'Teaism' now seems doubly alien to the rest of the world, describing as it does a tradition that is both peculiarly Japanese and more or less extinct. And yet, as I was to discover, the book is full of universal wisdom which its datedness cannot erase. Timeless, placeless truths always find their clearest expression in specific times and places. Religions revel in this paradox, welding the historical and the eternal with no apologies for the contradiction. It can be Jesus as God made man, the message of heaven for all humanity being sent to one man in Arabia, Vishnu becoming incarnate when humanity is in need. If there were a language of the infinite, finite human beings would not be able to understand it. Rooted in time and place, we need constantly to reframe our understanding of our condition in terms which speak to us as we are here and now.

So I came to realise that, for the truths contained in *The Book of Tea* to speak to us clearly today, its essence had to be distilled and blended into a different, contemporary concoction. To do that, it was necessary to take the tea out of Teaism. Superficially, this would appear to rip out its heart, like Christianity without Christ. In truth, the book could always have been about almost anything. The Japanese 'cult of tea' which Okakura called 'Teaism' is simply one manifestation of the Nipponese blend of Taoism and Zen Buddhism. In both, but Zen especially, there is no distinction between the big and the small, the important and the trivial, the sacred and the profane. The cosmos has a holographic pattern in which every part contains the whole.

The sublime can be seen as easily
in a cup of coffee as in an Alpine view,
if you know how to look.

The sublime can be seen as easily in a cup of coffee as in an Alpine view, if you know how to look.

Coffeeism is, in essence, the latest way of appreciating this core and essential truth. One becomes a devotee without even being a coffee drinker, just as one could be inspired by Okakura's Teaism without ever stepping inside a Japanese teahouse. Coffee culture is simply the best exemplar we have today for a philosophy for everyday life, a religion of the here and now that requires no gods or anything supernatural. And yet Teaism is not Coffeeism, at least not exactly. When Okakura set out the tenets of Teaism he was formalising a way of being that was already fully formed in his culture. There is as yet no such equivalent set of values and practices for Coffeeism. Still, the potential for Coffeeism can be found in the rituals and conventions of coffee drinking. It is a new iteration of an old philosophy, fumbling in the dark to find its full and truest expression.

The growth of coffee culture in the West reflects a yearning people may not even realise they have for a life that is at ease with itself, free from the fast-paced struggles of the modern world. The answers are on the tables and counters in front of them, but they can't see them because the West has no tradition of finding answers to the big questions in the smallest of things.

Teaism is Japan's gift to the West because it provides the basis for a Coffeeism. It allows the West to borrow the best Japanese values without requiring it to become something it is not.

It is even possible that Coffeeism could be the West's reciprocal present to Japan. For all its beauty and truth, Teaism is no longer fit for the hypermodern nation Japan has become. It is too nativist, too traditional, too inward-looking for a society that is now innovative and outward-looking. In Japan, too, coffee culture has taken off, perhaps as the Japanese look for something to revive the spirit of Teaism is a less ritualised, more cosmopolitan form.

To a Westerner, the idea of centring a worldview on a hot beverage can sound comical, pretentious or both. The Western imagination has been shaped by two powerful forces: Judaeo-Christian religion and ancient Greek philosophy. It has taken from both a disdain for the earthly, the temporal, the mundane, and has reserved its reverence for the eternal, the divine, the immaterial. Plato separated mind and body, and ever since, the majority of sages have praised the former and demeaned the latter.

Christianity began as a religion which allowed the body its importance, preaching the resurrection of the flesh. But as it absorbed Platonic influences it increasingly saw the corporeal as base and impure, placing its faith instead in the ultimate release of the soul.

In the Judaeo-Christian tradition, God reigns above in heaven, and all the time we are on this earth we are separated from him. If there was once a paradise on earth, Eden is no longer open to us. To return to the bosom of our creator we need to renounce

the flesh and its pleasures. As St Paul wrote, even having a family and children is second best to chastity, but since few are capable of this: 'It is better to marry than to burn' (1 Corinthians 7:9).

From childhood, Westerners are taught that what matters lies either beyond or in the grand life projects that take the place of transcendental religious values, such as family, career and material success. In such a culture, the mundane is not revered but reviled. To enjoy an everyday pleasure in passing is just about acceptable, but to elevate it to the meaning of life is decadent. It turns the cosmic order on its head. Yet such an inversion is exactly what the Western world needs, although it does not yet understand it. The West has already begun to worship the material and the transient but in entirely the wrong way. Our temples of pleasure are shopping malls and multiplexes, places of instant gratification but not of deep satisfaction. The West has climbed onto the hedonic treadmill, endlessly seeking pleasures and experiences and finding it has to run ever faster to get the same reward. It is restless, forever unsatisfied. For those who maintain the old religious ideals, this is a sign that it needs to return to its spiritual roots. The choice seems simple: shallow, meaningless materialism or transcendent, meaningful spirituality. The problem is that, if the former is unsatisfying, the latter seems implausible.

Coffeeism offers a way out of this existential impasse. It invites us to reject the dichotomy between the sacred and the profane. It suggests a spirituality which is focused on the immanent rather than the transcendent, the impermanent rather than the eternal, the material rather than the immaterial. In Japan, tea and its associated ceremonies once provided a way into this immanent spirituality, but there are, and have always been, innumerable other routes to the same destination. Coffee is as good as any other, and better than most.

Coffee's capacity to awaken within us a proper sense of the world and our place in it does not derive from some magical or chemical power. It is not a medicine or potion that works to cure us of our sickness of life by forcing upon us a transformation, whether we are willing to undertake it or not. Simply to drink coffee is not to follow the way of coffee. In order for coffee to heal us, we need to approach it in the right spirit.

Almost everyone instinctively has a sense of what this spirit is. In Britain, in times of crisis, the traditional response is the reassuringly banal and simple announcement: *I'll put the kettle on*. A tea or coffee can console more than words or empty hopes and promises. Advertisers have repeatedly latched on to the soothing capacity of a hot drink, selling us the idea of a moment of repose, tranquillity and simple, pure pleasure. With the

Coffeeism suggests a spirituality which is focused on the immanent rather than the transcendent, the impermanent rather than the eternal, the material rather than the immaterial.

warmth of a mug in our hand and a sip of its brown liquid, for a moment we are liberated from the ongoing struggle of daily life.

Okakura talked of this as a moment of finding 'beauty among the sordid facts of everyday life'. So many religions and philosophies promise salvation from the trouble and strife of life by taking us to something beyond it, be it heaven, unity with ultimate reality or achievement of a state of nirvana. Coffeeism has no time for such wishful thinking. It accepts with courageous honesty that we are of this world and have no escape from it. We have to live with its imperfections if we are to achieve any satisfaction. So instead of turning away from the world, squinting towards an eternal horizon far beyond our reach, the answer is to turn back to the world and to see what, amid all its tribulations, it can offer us in solace.

This demands that we look again at what we might have dismissed as trivial and unimportant and to see that, in fact, it is the textures of everyday life that gives it value. Western culture and education can smother our human nature only so much. Our rituals of coffee or tea drinking bear witness to our stubborn refusal to renounce the small consolations daily life offers.

Coffeeism does not promise perfection or completeness, and it is precisely this realism that makes it the ideal secular religion.

No one who says 'I'll put the kettle on' believes this will solve the problem or remove the heartache, and that is what gives the ritual cry its sincerity. The purpose is not to remove all the imperfections of life, which is impossible, but to help us to bear them. It is a reminder that, although life often seems impossible, it is possible to accomplish something good in it, however small, however fleeting. This is what we must cherish and hold on to if we are to withstand the slings and arrows of fortune.

Coffeeism offers not salvation but something that could etymologically have carried the same name. 'Salvation' derives from the Latin *salvare*, to save. In another possible world, it could have derived from the Old English *sealf*, 'healing ointment', the root of the modern word 'salve'. Coffeeism salves, it does not save, and in so doing it is superior to traditions that promise a salvation that is illusory and impossible.

In its mundanity, Coffeeism offers something that is relatively simple, cheap and available, rather than complex, costly and rare. This contrasts with the Western turn towards the mundane, in which things are valued in proportion to their scarcity, costliness or exceptionality. Faced with the prospect of mortality, people begin a desperate quest to tick off items on their bucket lists.

When it comes to the final reckoning, it is how we live day by day that matters more than how we live at rare, special moments.

Seeking gastronomic pleasure, they head for the new fashionable ingredient, luxury produce or exclusive restaurant. This gives us thrills but not contentment, bringing restlessness, not peace. Coffeeism does not deny the value of exceptional experiences but reminds us that we would be foolish to make their pursuit blind us to the beauties and delights that can be part of quotidian life. Is there a gourmand alive who would give up their preferred daily pleasures – coffee, tea, a glass of wine, a morning bowl of porridge – for the sake of their peak culinary experiences? If so, that would be a mistake.

When it comes to the final reckoning, it is how we live day by day that matters more than how we live at rare, special moments. When faced with terminal diagnoses, people's sense of what matters is often sharpened and they realise it is to be found in the good that surrounds them every day. This is what ultimately allows them to accept their own mortality. As Okakura put it, 'He only who has lived with the beautiful can die beautifully.'

Coffeeism also teaches us a proper humility, a correct sense of our place in the cosmos. Too many religions flatter us. Even as they scold us for our sinfulness, they tell us that our existence is of divine importance, that it is our destiny to abide in or with the eternal. Coffeeism tells us it is our destiny to live in the mortal frame in which we find ourselves only for so long as it holds out. It instructs us to seek meaning in the everyday because the everyday is all we have: we were not made for heaven.

To see supreme value in the smallest cup of coffee is not to inject the drink with an undeserved grandiosity but to deflate our own pomposity. If coffee is more important than we have thought, it is because we are less important than we have thought. The greatest artists, scientific geniuses, philosophers – none are above being cheered by the right drink or pleased by good food, and nor are they spared the excretory functions that follow. Reminded of this, the right response is not to despair but to laugh. Not the misanthropic laughter of the arrogant individual who sees themselves as above the rest of humanity but the affectionate laughter we direct at ourselves as members of a comic species. Anyone who cannot laugh at themselves takes themselves and life too seriously, and laughter not seriously enough.

To see our smallness for what it is is not to demean ourselves but to see 'the greatness of little things', to borrow another of Okakura's great little phrases.

Greatness is usually taken to be essentially connected with scale. To be great, something has to be of significance to many people, over a long period, across many miles. Greatness inspires awe, in which our own small existence becomes insignificant. Here again there is the dualistic dichotomy typical of Western thought: small and big, insignificant and awesome, major and minor. To break down these divisions we need to remember what it is like to be a child and to see the wonder in any blade of grass, leaf, worm or spider's web. Anyone who does not see as awesome the richness of life and the vitality of nature in any given square foot of land does not understand the awe of this world's larger spectacles. The wonder of life penetrates everything: it does not simply abide in the Himalayas, flow down the Amazon or erupt from Krakatoa.

Every cup of coffee is a source of wonder and amazement, one which we allow familiarity to dull. Each begins with a fruit grown the other side of the world. People with lives completely different from those who regularly sip flat whites pick the coffee berries, extract the bean within and dry them. By truck and by ship, they are sent on a journey across the widest oceans. The beans are roasted and ground, and somehow that distant fruit is transformed into a drink with a unique set of characteristics. A different bean, a different roast, a different preparation and it would have been a different drink. And, most remarkably of all, you, a creature of consciousness and self-consciousness, absorb this drink into your own body, smelling, tasting, digesting, excreting. Because you exist, there is a whole world of experience that centres on you and your subjectivity. And yet there are also billions of other such worlds, other centres of experience, coming and going in and out of existence all the time, all part of a fecund world where each life is connected with every other. A whole universe, with billions of years of evolution, had to exist to make that sip of the drink possible. Every breath we take is an unimaginably unlikely miracle, one that owes nothing to divine intervention or fate's hand, but everything to blind chance.

The great is little, the little is great. To understand this is to be humble about ourselves and to be properly appreciative of the qualities of others. To put Okakura's great little phrase in context, he said, 'those who cannot feel the littleness of great things in themselves are apt to overlook the greatness of little things in others'. To focus on the mundane is not to narrow one's vision but to expand it. To see the wonder in the part is to see more clearly the wonder in the whole. Wars and conflicts are made possible by a view of the world in which only the large is visible: the march of history, the destiny of humankind, the fates of nations. In such a perspective, the loss of a thousand or so lives, the destruction of a town or two, are of small consequence. When we see that all that matters can be found in a single home, a single life, war and destruction becomes unconscionable. One cup of coffee left undrunk because the soldier did not return home is enough to expose the hollowness of the grandiose narratives of conquerors.

I see now why it is so fitting that I didn't buy *The Book of Tea* when I first found it. A common trope of myth and fiction is the hero who does not heed the call when he first hears it. The call has more stamina than strength; it wins by persistence, not brute force. The call of Coffeeism has the same character, but without the aggrandising nonsense of myth. I was not being called that day on to a grand quest, and I will never be any kind of hero. Rather, I have heard an incessant whisper, telling me that if I am to have any success in life it must be achieved by embracing and not denying the smallness and the shortness of my existence. This is a reverse mythology, in which it is only by giving up the fantasy of a heroic quest that we can fully embrace our destinies.

# ii
# Tao and Zen

Coffeeism is rooted in Teaism which was, in turn, rooted in Tao and Zen. The Zen and Taoist roots of Coffeeism still matter, but we need not worry about whether its present-day flowering is true to its authentic seeds. Okakura warned against 'slavish conformity to traditions and formulas'. We should not abandon the creations of the past but seek to make them 'true to contemporaneous life' rather than to preserve them as dead museum pieces.

The idea of a true, original religion is in any case a misguided and dangerous one. It is ironic that self-proclaimed defenders of religion deny their exalted faiths the capacity of growth which even the humblest weed possesses. Zen itself is a late variant of a much older Buddhism. What matters when religions evolve is not that we retain what is oldest in them but what is truest.

Both Taoism and Zen contain many truths that stand on their own feet outside their traditions. These are truths which in many ways secular Japanese society has lived by. Chief among them is a fundamental individualism. This will surprise those who believe Japan to be the conformist society par excellence, but only because they assume Western individualism is the only kind there is.

The individualism of the East is phenomenological. That is to say, it is based on the insight that reality for each of us is limited to what falls within our consciousness. Mind exists before matter, in that, without mind, there cannot be any experience of matter. Hence the basic principle: attend first and most carefully to your own consciousness, if you are to understand yourself and the world.

This idea came rather later to Europe in the late nineteenth and early twentieth century under the name of phenomenology. Indeed, to describe the core idea these mainly German and French philosophers shared would require no more than a repetition of the preceding paragraph. It has even been suggested that the early phenomenologists were directly inspired by Asian philosophers they failed to acknowledge. The parallels between Martin Heidegger's concept of *Dasein* (being in the world) and Kakuzo's description of one of the central ideas of the fourth-century BCE Chinese philosopher Zhuangzi as 'being in the world' (*das-in-der-Welt-sein* in German) are certainly striking. The possibility that this is mere coincidence is reduced somewhat by the fact that Kakuzo's student Tomonobu Imamichi (1922–2012) claimed his teacher gave a copy of *The Book of Tea* to Heidegger in 1919. If true, Heidegger's fault was not that he stole wisdom that was freely given, merely that he failed to show gratitude for the gift.

To appreciate the primacy of each individual's phenomenology, nothing more is needed than your attention and something to attend to, such as a cup of coffee taken in a garden. Sitting down to drink it, you have a background sense of being located in a much wider world. Attend to that world. Every characteristic it has is actually a characteristic of your consciousness. The coffee is only that shade of brown to your eyes; it is only that warm to your touch. Offer a taste to someone else and their experience will not be exactly the same as yours.

Meditate upon this, look around you and you will observe a miracle. A whole universe exists solely because you experience it. When you die, that world dies with you, collapsing to nothing like the space inside a burst balloon. The sun may be the centre of the solar system, but you are the centre of the universe you inhabit.

It is thought that the eighteenth-century idealist philosophy of George Berkeley (1685–1753) first provoked the question: 'If a tree falls in an empty forest, does it make a sound?' Those who do not understand the enduring power of this dismiss it, believing that obviously things happen in this universe unobserved. Of course they do. The real question is whether we can say anything sensible about what such mind-independent reality is like in itself. For sure, when a tree crashes, something is

happening whether we see it or not. But only from a particular point of view is it *a tree crashing*. From the perspective of physics, a certain arrangement of atoms becomes a somewhat different arrangement of atoms, and there is no need to talk of trees or sounds. Physics is, however, a human science, and we have no idea whether it maps onto ultimate science, whatever that might be.

This is the lesson of the story of Hui-neng (638–713), the founder of Zen, who passed two monks arguing about the temple flag waving in the wind. One claimed the flag moved, the other that the wind moved. Hui-neng told them they were both wrong: 'It is not the wind that moves; it is not the flag that moves; it is your mind that moves.' There cannot be any perception of a flag waving in the wind, nor any conception of flags, wind and movement, without a mind to observe them, to frame reality in a way that makes such talk possible. This is the individualism of Zen: the absolute centrality of consciousness. Attend to this individuality more closely, however, and something remarkable happens: you vanish.

Observe the cup of coffee and carefully note everything you experience: the sight of the smooth white ceramic surface of the cup; the warmth of its sides as you cup it in your hands; the wonderful scent of roasted beans, which may be more delightful

You are an ordered collection
of body parts and your conscious life
a (more or less) ordered collection
of conscious experiences. If you try to
peer behind these for a 'you',
you will find nothing.

than the slightly bitter, nutty taste of the drink as it moistens your mouth and passes through your throat; the pleasure and feeling of well-being the whole experience generates. The list could go on but there is something it will never contain: the experience of the you having the experience. Common sense tells you that there is something behind all of this, the 'you' having the experience. Careful introspection shows this to be false: there is nothing but the experiences themselves. You exist only as the sum of their parts.

To those unused to attentive self-consciousness, such a thought can be surprising and alarming. This is itself surprising and shows an alarming lack of self-awareness in human beings as they go about their lives. Those surprised that they are no more than the sum of their parts have failed to notice that everything else in the universe is the sum of *its* parts. Why should we be any exception? The coffee you imbibe is nothing more than a collection of hydrogen and oxygen atoms, infused with the soluble compounds of the coffee bean. The porcelain cup you drink it out of is a fused blend of hydrous aluminium silicate and quartz. You, in turn, are an ordered collection of body parts and your conscious life a (more or less) ordered collection of conscious experiences. If you try to peer behind these for a 'you', you will find nothing.

The self is empty, and we should be glad it is. Imagine that we were each discrete individual atoms of existence, pearls of selfhood bouncing around in a vast, cold universe. What a fate, to be so utterly separated from others, alone in our egos, peering through the windows of our souls but unable ever to get out, or to let anyone in. What a blessing it is instead to be without a hard shell, an impenetrable core, and to instead to be a field of being, a nexus of experiences. Such fluid, unbounded selves have the capacity to overlap and connect with other similarly amorphous beings in the ongoing dance of experience we call life. Each of us is a collection of experiences in an infinitely vaster collection of experiences.

Remarkably, we thus find that a philosophy which is rooted in the most radical individualism is precisely the philosophy that delivers us from radical solipsism. We discover that, far from existing only as atomic selves, we exist only as interrelated ones. The self is not atomic but relational. Who we are is defined by our relations to others and to the world.

Again, this is an insight which is both profound and completely mundane. Ask anyone to define their identity and they always do so by listing those they are related to, the groups to which they belong: father, son, brother, Japanese, Buddhist, liberal, chef. Those who resist this and call themselves only 'outsiders' or 'individuals' fail to see the irony that these identities are also relational, defining us by the groups we refuse to belong to.

A relational understanding of the self is desperately needed in the West, where individualism is worshipped without being understood. Western individualism constantly undermines itself. People seek individualism by personalising themselves and their possessions in exactly the same way that others do. A tattoo's uniqueness is less significant than the fact that the tattooed are far from unique. No amount of customisation can disguise the fact that we have the same phone as millions of others. People seek individuality to stand out from the crowd, but this goal only makes sense if the crowd's attention is an important source of value.

But what is the alternative? Conformity? It should first be pointed out that Western individualism is itself a source of remarkable conformity. All those American East Coast liberal individuals look as alike to an outsider as the Japanese are thought to look to Westerners. So, too, do they think alike on all sorts of issues such as multiculturalism, the evils of the global capitalism they nonetheless profit from, the rights of whales, women's liberation, democracy. Western individuals who fail to see how deeply they conform with the norms and values of their ilk are comic, pitiful creatures.

The antidote to this ersatz individualism is not another kind of conformity but an individualism that fully recognises that to be a self, one has to be socially located. To be an individual is to play your part in the whole, and that can only be done if you see that you are indeed part of a whole.

Observe your neighbourhood barista. Do not do so with the complacent modern, Western idealisation of the individual exemplified by French Existentialist Jean-Paul Sartre (1905–80). Watching his contemporary counterpart of the barista, a waiter, Sartre was filled with disdain for the way in which this apparently deluded figure so inhabited his role that he lost all sense of his individuality. The waiter, thought Sartre, lived in bad faith, denying his own freedom and agency, pretending instead that he was merely doing what waiters do.

Perhaps this particular waiter had indeed given up his agency. But Sartre's attitude has endured in ways that owe nothing to the careful psychological observation of individuals and everything to do with a prejudicial dismissal of anyone who dares to play a part in a larger drama they are neither writing nor directing. We talk of them as 'cogs in a machine', rodents running in a rat race. The language is deliberately dehumanising, because we cannot imagine how one can both be human and give up so much of oneself to 'the system'.

Try observing the barista once again, with more sympathy. Of course she is not a senseless automaton, a mindless zombie who has subsumed herself entirely to an impersonal capitalist system that exploits her labour for no other purpose than profit. When she leaves work she will go and do the same kinds of things that you do. Her life is one of love, friendship, struggle, sickness, meaningful experiences, learning, simple pleasures and exceptional adventures. Does she then lead a double life, turning herself into a barista-bot for forty hours a week? No. If she is no more than a cog in a machine, then so are you, merely one of the pennies popped into the slot to keep the machine running.

In a technologically advanced consumer society, we can all too easily slide into a way of viewing the world in which other people become just executors of functions and the things of the world mere resources. The problem is not that the system demands this but that it encourages it, and we are too easily led. It is not the world that needs to change but how we see it. It is up to us to refuse to dehumanise our daily interactions, to see others as selves not functionaries.

The battle is not between protecting our individuality and giving in to 'the system'. It is in seeing the system for what it is: a network of human activity. Perhaps our barista has recognised, even if only implicitly, that to be a true individual in this world you have to find a unique place in it and play your part, like a piece of a jigsaw. The customer is not greater than the barista, the barista is not greater than the roaster, the roaster not greater than the grower. Each should recognise that they are at the same time of equal importance and of equal smallness in the mundane drama of social life in which each plays their part. To perform our role we need to know our own part inside out, and we cannot know that unless we keep in mind the ongoing soap opera in which we participate. There is then no forced choice between subsuming your identity to the herd or roaming alone. It is only in relation to others that our own distinctiveness can come out.

If our barista is a true coffee master, she does her work with dignity, knowing that every link in the chain that brings coffee to our lips is essential and that none is greater than her own part or lesser than the whole to which she contributes. This is the spirit in which the traveller is often surprised to find everyone does their work in Japan. The culture has taken from Zen – or perhaps Zen has taken from the culture – the idea that no task is in itself more important than another. What matters is not *what* is done, but *how* it is done. In a Zen monastery, all tasks are shared and all are done with equal attention and care, from washing vegetables to cleaning the floor. Some

The culture has taken from Zen – or perhaps Zen has taken from the culture – the idea that no task is in itself more important than another. What matters is not *what* is done, but *how* it is done.

of the most menial work (by Western standards) is done by the most senior monks.

If this spirit is lost in many who do the work of baristas in the West, it is not due to the nature of their task. Sometimes, the barista believes erroneously that the job is beneath them, and so they fulfil their duties without attention, meeting the minimum standards to avoid being fired and no more. This feeling is often fostered by a management which fails to respect the most important people in the business and by a society that fails to respect craft when it sees it.

To be cured of these prejudices, there is nothing better than a visit to an independent craft coffee shop. The best baristas there approach their task like true Japanese *shokunin*, a master craftsperson, treating every shot with equal seriousness, always trying to produce the perfect cup. They work with calm concentration, in a kind of meditative state. With time and practice, they enter a state of flow in which their mastery enables them to completely immerse themselves in their work and to experience that heightened sense of satisfaction that comes when one's skill is perfectly matched to the task.

This has a lot in common with what the Taoists call *wu wei*. This is a kind of effortless, natural action that meets no resistance.

The paradox of *wu wei* is that it can be achieved only with great difficulty. We have to undergo a long period of effortful practice in order to emerge at the end of the process able to perform the task almost without thinking at all. This is not the Western sense of doing something thoughtlessly, which implies lack of attention and carelessness. *Wu wei* is a kind of unthinking action that is attentive and mindful but requires no calculation or deliberation.

Many Westerners will nod approvingly when talking about such exotic ideas as *wu wei*, but when they observe them in action in more familiar surroundings, their apparent respect quickly disappears. Dedicated baristas are often mocked for the earnestness of their 'obsession', as though there were something obviously wrong about taking such a small task so seriously. Those who mock ought to ask themselves what makes their own occupations so cosmically important. In the grand scheme of things, we are all doing small work. We can make it great only by doing it with greatness of heart and mind.

This requires us to approach the secular world with a religious seriousness. Okakura describes Teaism as a 'religion of the art of life'. Coffeeism is another denomination of the same faith, and like all religions it has its own founding myth. Around a century after the death of the Prophet Muhammad, an Ethiopian goatherd named Kaldi noticed that his beasts became decidedly frisky after they had eaten the bright berries of a particular bush. Curious, he chewed a few himself, arousing a state of exhilaration. Keen to understand the nature of this strange berry, he took some to a Sufi monk who, suspicious of their seemingly demonic power, threw them on the fire. But as they roasted there, a beautiful aroma filled the room. When the fire died down, the monk pulled out the beans, ground them, mixed them with water and made the first cup of coffee.

Like all myths, historical accuracy is irrelevant to this tale's truth. Coffeeism does not have anything so grand or formal as doctrines, but the story does capture many of its key insights. It is no accident that this is a story of genuinely humble origins. All religions speak of humility, but few exhibit it. Even the birth of the messiah in a manger involves celestial guidance, an entourage of angels, the homage of wealthy kings. In this tale we have nothing more than a peasant, a bush and some goats. The hero has no great qualities except a keen observation of the familiar world around him and a curiosity, and yet these are the only qualities needed by a philosopher or scientist: watch, ask, test.

It is also fitting that the monk is shown to be prejudiced, initially blinded to the potential value of the fruit he is brought.

How often does religion lead to a closing of minds rather than an opening of them to the full wonder of the universe? The monk's orientation towards the transcendent makes him downright hostile to the immanent value of the coffee. But we are all ultimately pulled down to earth, no matter how hard we try to ascend to heaven. The smell of the roasting beans is too alluring to be ignored.

Not that the monk allows himself to admit he could be swayed by such secular concerns. He ultimately endorses the consumption of coffee because it helps him stay awake longer, all the better to pray more. We may smile and allow him to cloak his enjoyment of the everyday in the guise of devotion to the eternal, confident that, at the moment each drink touches his lips, he is right here and now with the rest of us. The goatherd, connected as he is with the land and the passage of the seasons, needs no such rationalisation.

We may also smile at the role human ingenuity plays in this myth. Coffee is a gift from nature, but one which we need to work on in order to transform it into the drink we love. We may flatter ourselves for our ability to achieve this alchemy, but what we call human ingenuity is often little more than all-too-human accident. Coffee began with a mistake of throwing away the beans in the one place that happened to be bring out their fullest potential. Can there be any better myth for a religion which revels in our imperfection?

The tale of Kaldi suggests a subtle but important difference between Teaism and Coffeeism (which are after all two branches of the same essential faith). Teaism is rooted in religion. The tea ceremony evolved from a Zen ritual in which monks drank from a single bowl of tea before an image of Bodhidharma (fl. sixth century CE), the founder of Chan Buddhism, as Zen was first known in China. Both Zen and Taoism have a healthy disregard for many of the traditional trappings of religion. One of the most famous Zen koans, attributed to the Chan Buddhist Linji Yixuan (d. 866), is: 'If you meet the Buddha, kill him.' This is, of course, not meant literally, but is a kind of warning against taking any kind of religious instruction on authority.

If Teaism moves us to the fringes of religion, Coffeeism takes us more or less out of it, or at least to the point at which distinctions between religion and philosophy, the sacred and the profane, become irrelevant. Coffeeism is constructed neither on a foundation of rational argument nor on tenets of faith or revelation. It is rooted in reverence for the material universe, not some heavenly other. It stands or falls on whether it speaks to our needs and sense of who we are, things which are not exempt from the scrutiny of rationality but which cannot

Coffeeism is constructed neither
on a foundation of rational argument
nor on tenets of faith or revelation.
It is rooted in reverence for
the material universe,
not some heavenly other.

be entirely justified by reason, either. It is religious in form but secular in its contents.

Coffee has always had an ambivalent relationship with religion. The Ethiopian monk was not the only cleric to be suspicious of its powers to stimulate the flesh. In the Islamic world, where alcohol was prohibited, coffee became the mild intoxicant of choice. Its Arabic name, *quawah* (the etymological origin of many languages' word for coffee, including English), originally meant 'wine'. This made Christendom suspicious of this heathen beverage, which some dismissed as 'Satan's drink'. Some advisors to Pope Clement VIII (r. 1592–1605) even wanted him to ban it, but he refused to do so before trying it himself. When he did, legend says he declared, 'This devil's drink is delicious. We should cheat the devil by baptising it.'

Such suspicion might seem comical today, when coffee mornings are a ubiquitous feature of church life. Only the religious texts of the Church of Jesus Christ of Latter-day Saints, more commonly known as the Mormon Church, prohibit the consumption of hot drinks, interpreted as meaning tea and coffee. Nonetheless, the scent of sin seems never to have been too far away from coffee. It certainly wafted from the coffeehouses of seventeenth- and eighteenth-century Britain. In part, this had nothing to do with the coffee and everything to do with the seditious talk such establishments appeared to foster. In 1675, King Charles II (r. 1660–85) even issued 'A proclamation for the suppression of the coffee-houses', saying that they attracted 'idle and disaffected persons' by whom 'diverse False, Malitious and Scandalous Reports are devised and spread abroad, to the Defamation of His Majesties Government, and to the Disturbance of the Peace and Quiet of the Realm'.

Often, however, the negative effects of the coffeehouses were attributed to the drink itself. A year before King Charles's ultimately abortive attempt at suppression, 'the women's petition against coffee' was presented to the public by some concerned residents of London. The petition decried the 'excessive use of that Newfangled, Abominable, Heathenish Liquor called COFFEE, which Riffling Nature of her Choicest Treasures, and Drying up the Radical Moisture, has so Eunucht our Husbands, and Crippled our more kind Gallants, that they are become as Impotent, as Age, and as unfruitful as those Desarts whence that unhappy Berry is said to be brought'. Coffee was thought to be enfeebling, not least sexually: 'They come from it with nothing moist but their snotty Noses, nothing stiffe but their Joints, nor standing but their Ears. [...] A Betrothed Queen might trust her self a bed with one of them, without the nice Caution of a Sword between them.'

Coffee exposes our tethers to our animality but in a way which we find positive and pleasurable.

The petition was surely satirical, but one which exaggerated and reflected real concerns expressed in other contemporaneous writings.

Coffee is always unsettling for religious moralists because it proves how dependent even our mental functioning is on the simple matter of what we ingest. At the same time, it is too benign in its effects to generate deep concern in the general populace. Coffee exposes our tethers to our animality but in a way which we find positive and pleasurable. That makes it a much more devious enemy for those who imagine us to be temporarily embodied spirits than stronger intoxicants whose deleterious effects are undeniable.

As with all intoxicants, advocates of coffee do not deny its effects on the mind and body but insist they are positive. Coffee's medicinal properties have always been disputed. The seventeenth-century French apothecary Philippe Sylvestre Dufour claimed that the first recorded mention of coffee came in the writings of the Persian physician and philosopher Abu Bakr al-Razi (also known by his Latinised name Rhazes; c. 865–925/35), who described *buncham* (another Arabic name for the drink derived from *bunn*, the coffee berry) as 'hot and dry and good for the stomach'. Two centuries later Ibn Sina (Avicenna; d. 1037) mentioned it in the pharmacopoeia that completed his

*Canon of Medicine*. One Oxford coffee seller declared in 1660 that coffee had so many beneficial effects that 'it would be too tedious to nominate everything it is good for'. In 1721, coffee was also credited with stopping the spread of bubonic plague.

Today, the debate still ebbs and flows, with coffee said to be a cause of cancer on some days, and to slow dementia on others. True devotees of Coffeeism should not be so tribal as to take one side on this dispute. If coffee has any medicinal benefits, we'll take them, but that is not why coffeeistas drink it. If coffee has any negative effects, so be it: is there anything in this world that is entirely good or bad?

The runner whose exercise strengthens her heart may nonetheless be struck by a heart attack when pushing herself too far, and is almost certainly grinding away at her joints, hampering her future mobility. Coffee gives health benefits with one hand and takes others away with the other. We may one day know exactly how much this leaves us in credit or debit, but given that we have no reason to believe it is either a poison or the elixir of life, it would be inappropriate to worry too much about it.

Coffeeism is about accepting our place in the world as mortals who never know how much time we have left. We can influence

If coffee has any negative effects,
so be it: is there anything
in this world that is entirely
good or bad?

but not control the length of our lives, and wisdom lies in knowing when to try and when to leave it to chance. When we drink our coffee, we resign ourselves to that which we have no choice but to resign ourselves to.

For this reason, the coffee snob is no true disciple of Coffeeism. In his remarkable *Instructions to the Zen Cook* the Japanese monk Dōgen (1200–53) tells us that 'a dish is not necessarily superior because you have prepared it with choice ingredients, nor is a soup inferior because you have made it with ordinary greens'. We have to make the most of whatever is available, and this requires treating the plainest ingredient with the same respect as the most rare and refined. It also means receiving whatever is offered to us in the same spirit of gratitude, whether it is a mug of instant coffee or a flat white from the world barista champion. The connoisseur who can abide only the best has become a slave to his passion, unable to function with anything less than the finest. His strength becomes a weakness, an ability to discern an inability to adapt.

Coffeeism always takes a realistic attitude to life. The Buddhists say that we are too attached to our material existence, that we cling too much to worldly, mortal goods. Coffeeism shows that there is a way to embrace life without clinging to it, like a lover whose tenderness never slips into a stifling possessiveness.

Coffeeism revels in the blessings of every day, but always accepts them for what they are: fleeting, impermanent, brief. It wears the smile of one who has been treated to the sight of a kingfisher by the water, watching it fly away, grateful for the moment of magic it gave, not resentful that it has now passed.

# iii
# Flowers

Traditional Japanese tea rooms were free from adornment, save for a calligraphy scroll or brush painting and a simple flower arrangement. This creates the feel of a shrine or temple, an atmosphere of quiet reverence. But reverence for what? Reverence for the beauty of the world and its transience.

The religion of Teaism is a religion of aestheticism, based on the worship of the simple beauty of daily life. It is thereby a religion of the immanent, of the here and now, not the transcendent, the otherworldly and the eternal. In this its connection with Taoism is evident. Taoism, says Okakura, is the 'art of being in the world'. Taoism is often described as a religion of nature, but this is misleading to Western ears, for whom nature is often thought of as outside the human. In Taoism, nature is exactly the same as what we would simply call the world. Buildings, machines, works of art: everything human-made is as much part of nature as the plants and animals that populate wild forests. Taoism accepts the totality of the world as the totality of all that is, and in this Teaism and Coffeeism follow.

The combination of flower, artwork and teahouse expresses this perfectly. Everything is made from what we call natural materials, which really means materials more closely and clearly related to their natural origins than the likes of plastic, steel and concrete. These human-made materials are equally made from elements drawn from the ground but have been so metamorphosed that their connection with it is easily forgotten or missed.

In the teahouse, nature and artifice exist in perfect balance. Tea is cultivated and processed to create a drink drawn from the natural environment but not found in it. The painting will likely depict a scene from nature rather than of a person, yet it was made by a person. The flowers are both purely natural but cut and arranged in an entirely artificial way. Unlike the ostentatious bouquets so loved in the West, these flower arrangements are very simple and may comprise just a single flower. A bouquet proudly boasts of the wealth of its purchaser and their capacity to take so much from nature. In contrast, Japanese flowers whisper of the arranger's sensitivity and fine taste and his unwillingness to take no more life from the fertile canvas of the soil than is strictly necessary. Whereas the bouquet is about human domination of the flower fields, a simple, small arrangement is about harmony with it. The skill of the Japanese arranger is in allowing the beauty of each flower to show itself in its fullest glory.

In a Western bouquet, the bigger the arrangement, the more each individual flower is lost in the whole. Once again, it is the West which is revealed to have the lesser true individualism and the East where each part is more clearly discernible and given space to be itself. In the West, more is more, until all that is of special value is lost in the jumble of possessions and experiences greedily accumulated. In the East, less is more, since it is only by giving fewer things their proper attention that anything can have any value at all.

Above all, the flower stands for all the beauty which is transient in the world, which is all the beauty that there is. The moment a flower is cut it begins to die. To admire a cut flower is to admire beautiful decay. In Japanese aesthetics, this is described in terms of *wabi-sabi*, an attitude not just of acceptance but appreciation for impermanence and imperfection.

Although contemporary coffeehouses often make space for a few plants, the flower clearly does not have the central role in

Coffee culture reiterates anew
the ethos of the flower arrangement
in its embrace of *wabi-sabi*.
Coffee of its nature provides
fleeting pleasure.

contemporary Coffeeism that it had in tea culture. But many share the traditional Japanese fascination with finding harmony between what nature gives and what we make of it. There is a widespread use of natural materials, from exposed brick walls to reclaimed-wood surfaces. But there is also a lot of metal, from steel table legs to the stainless steel and chrome of the espresso machine. Most obviously, coffee itself is at once something that grows from the land and becomes no less natural because it requires technology and human processing to be turned into a drink. Capturing its natural flavours requires skill and effort. Nature doesn't simply give; it requires us to contribute to bring out its potential.

Another way in which coffee culture reiterates anew the ethos of the flower arrangement in its embrace of *wabi-sabi*. Coffee of its nature provides fleeting pleasure. At its extreme, the espresso is devoured in mere seconds. It has taken a long time for people from other beverage cultures to understand this. Not so long ago, there were places in Britain where, if you asked for an espresso, the server would check whether you realised it was 'the really small one', on the assumption that the vast majority of people would find paying for such a drink a poor bargain. The retort of the espresso drinker is to ask what manner of desperation would motivate anyone to be so keen to drag out what is always going to be a relatively brief drinking experience anyway. In trying to protract the moment, we betray an unwillingness to accept that it is indeed just a moment, a blinking of the cosmic eye.

Similarly, many protest that their coffee is not served piping hot, when coffeeistas know that the best temperature to bring out the flavours is much cooler, meaning that, once served, it cannot sit too long. Hence the drinker of the long, piping-hot coffee is trying too hard to cling to the moment, while the downer of the espresso is cheerfully embracing the shortness both of life and any happiness found within it.

For those who consume coffee as a commodity, something that comes out of a packet, intimations of transience are limited to the experience of drinking itself. For those more mindful of coffee as a plant that has been processed, transience infuses every bean. The whole cycle of coffee production and consumption is one of impermanence, life and death.

It starts with the plant, most commonly the species *Coffea arabica*, from which around sixty per cent of the world's coffee is harvested. It takes three to four years of growth before the plant produces berries and seven for it to fully mature, after which it will have another thirteen years of good productivity. It could live to a hundred, but few farmers would allow it such a long period of semi-retirement. There is therefore a roughly twenty-year cycle of birth, growth and death, turning everywhere coffee is grown.

A handful of beans will be germinated to keep the cycle of growth rotating. Most, however, must be killed. To do this requires stripping them of three layers of protective husk, the exocarp, mesocarp and endocarp. Traditionally, this was done first by drying them in the sun and then hulling the beans mechanically, by anything from millstones to state-of-the-art steel machinery. Increasingly, producers use the 'wet method', where beans are soaked, fermented and washed to remove any pulp and the first two layers of husk, before hulling removes the remaining endocarp. These 'green beans' are then cleaned, polished and sorted before being sold on to roasters, semi-cremating these already-dead corpses. Finally, the beans are ground – ashes to ashes, dust to dust.

And yet, once brewed, the beans have the capacity to give life once more. This is not because they provide energy: coffee contains virtually no calories. It does nonetheless invigorate, by virtue of the stimulant caffeine it contains. This is, of course, also found in tea, providing a further link between Teaism and Coffeeism. Increasingly, there is a consensus that on balance coffee provides positive health benefits, offering some protection against type 2 diabetes, being good for your heart and liver, and protecting against cancer. This reverses an earlier view that coffee was in fact a carcinogen. In fact, the cancer risk from coffee is only significant if you drink it in unfeasibly large quantities or too hot: a prudential reason to drink it cooler to add to the aesthetic one.

The ultimate destiny of coffee is, however, back to the earth, the drink expelled in urine, and the grounds returned to the soil. Absurdly, we think of both of these as waste or byproducts. Used properly, neither is waste and neither is a mere byproduct. A byproduct is incidental to the core process of production, something that is not part of a cycle but is cast off into its own digressive cul-de-sac. Nature has no byproducts, for everything either has its use and place in the grand scheme of thing, or else it fails the selection test of evolution and becomes extinct.

Things are only byproducts from the perspective of creatures who privilege what is of direct use to them and see anything else as irrelevant. To drink coffee mindful of its true nature is therefore to connect with the transience of life and death. And yet because this is a cycle, it is without beginning or end.

Strictly speaking, it is not eternal, since the universe itself emanated from a big bang and one day will almost certainly extinguish to oblivion. Still, to a human, the difference between eternity and billions of years is irrelevant. Both are unimaginably vaster than ourselves, utterly beyond our comprehension in anything more than a purely abstract, theoretical sense. So it transpires that connecting with the impermanence of all things also allows us to connect with an as-good-as-endless cycle and so to ride on the back of eternity. By being completely in the bounded present, we locate ourselves properly in the boundless past and future.

The connections we forge by our partaking of coffee are spatial as well as temporal. When we are fully mindful of what we are drinking, we see that it connects us with the sun, the rains, the soil, the seasons, technology, people on the other side of the globe. It takes a remarkably advanced and interconnected world to make our simple daily brew. Recognising this enlarges our perspectives and shows how small the space from which we view it really is.

Although the *wabi-sabi* spirit of the tearoom flower persists in the modern coffeehouse, there is another way on which it is far removed. The flower played a part which was wordless. How this contrasts to the more typical adornments of the contemporary café: books, magazines, newspapers. The stereotypical habitué of the café is a bookish sort, immersed in reading or writing. Indeed, many cafés are more famous for what was written than drunk there. J K Rowling wrote much of *Harry Potter and the Philosopher's Stone* at The Elephant House in Edinburgh; French Existentialists Simone de Beauvoir and Jean-Paul Sartre composed many of their works at Paris's left-bank Café de Flore; Ernest Hemingway wrote – and drank – at the Café Iruña in Pamplona.

Such an emphasis on words is anathema to the spirit both of Taoism and Zen. Okakura said that in Zen 'words are but an

When we are fully mindful of what we are drinking, we see that it connects us with the sun, the rains, the soil, the seasons, technology, people on the other side of the globe.

encumbrance to thought'. Language stands in the way of 'direct communion with the inner nature of things'. One of the main purposes of apparently nonsensical koans, such as 'What is the colour of wind?' or 'When the many are reduced to one, to what is the one reduced?', is to make us see the limitations of language. When we mediate the world through concepts, we can easily be led to nonsense that looks like sense because they are linked in grammatical chains.

Another problem with words is that they create the illusion of solidity and permanence when everything is transient and impermanent. Knowledge in the West is transmitted primarily through texts; wisdom in the East by discipleship from a respected master. Knowledge can persist unknown to any person in the books of a library; wisdom dies unless it lives actively in a human mind.

In the West, understanding is mediated primarily through language; in the East, through experience. Both provide kinds of knowledge, *logos* being knowledge through words, *gnosis* knowledge through direct experience. That does not mean experience doesn't matter in the West or that language doesn't matter in the East. It is simply a question of what matters most.

Coffeeism should be sufficiently ecumenical to accommodate these differences in emphasis. The West's preference for *logos* should be seen neither as a weakness nor a strength, merely a characteristic. Let us not strip a café of its reading material in a misguided attempt to make it more like the East. Let us instead embrace all that the café has to offer the dedicated coffeeista.

# iv
# The Café

The café as a site of reading and writing appears primarily as a site of *logos*. For as long as cafés have existed, they have been associated with words, learning and philosophy. The earliest coffeehouses in Arabia were so well known as places of intellectual exchange that they were known as 'schools of the Wise'. When cafés conquered Europe in the seventeenth century, their association with free thought was so strong that many thought them dangerous. In England, they became known as 'penny universities', the price of a coffee being all you needed for hours of edifying conversation. There might have been no twentieth-century French Existentialism were it not for the endless discussions conducted in Parisian cafés.

Nonetheless, cafés also provide ample opportunities for *gnosis*. Prime among these is what many refer to as *people watching*. Cafés are especially suited to this because they are one of the few public spaces where solitude can be enjoyed without fear of suspicion or stigmatisation. A café provides a licence to simply abide and observe.

Such observation extends to the morally problematic matter of eavesdropping. We are taught that this is the height of rudeness, but it is almost as though the café has been designed to encourage it. Tables are usually close enough together that it requires effort *not* to hear what your neighbours are saying rather than to tune in. Nor do those neighbours usually make much effort to keep their voices to themselves. You can hear the most intimate issues being discussed as though people were in the privacy of their own homes when they know they are not. It is almost as though when we enter a café we make a deal: you may eavesdrop on me if I, in turn, can eavesdrop on others.

If such a pact does not exist then it ought to. We may look to fiction and art to understand our fellow human beings, but an hour in a café can generate more insight than the same time spent bent over a novel. I suspect that this is why so many people take books to cafés: they know they will probably not be able to concentrate but they also know what will distract them will be more interesting than what they are reading anyway, and the book at least provides the cover of pretending to be absorbed in something else.

In most parts of the world, others would know what that something else was. Not in Japan. Nobody there knew when I was reading *The Book of Tea* because when I bought it the bookseller wrapped its cover with the shop's own decorative paper, as is the custom in Japan. Some misinformed Westerners repeat the scurrilous urban myth that this is because many adults in Japan read teenage manga comics, and this spares them their blushes. The truth is the custom predates this fashion. Decorum and modesty mean that it is considered inappropriate to broadcast whatever you are reading. It may be embarrassing to be seen reading a manga, but it could also be considered a form of boasting to advertise that you were a *literatus* devouring Murakami or Mishima. Whatever you are reading, it is between you and the book, and such intimacy is not for the public square.

I say deliberately that this is a question of intimacy and not privacy. It is very natural for Westerners to characterise many differences as between public and private when other distinctions are available. Take the fact that the tearoom is a domestic setting whereas the café is a public one. Nonetheless, in some ways the café is a more private space than the tearoom. In the café, an individual may retreat into her own inner world, ignoring everyone around her. Despite the implicit invitation to eavesdrop, conversations are officially private, and to interrupt one with your own contribution would be the

The best cafés are perhaps those that manage to provide both privacy and intimacy when wanted. They are places both for dignified solitude and civilised discussion.

height of rudeness. The café allows its guests both anonymity and privacy. In the tearoom, however, everyone participates in the ceremony together, giving everyone else full attention. No one is allowed a moment purely to themselves. The event is not public but is better described as intimate rather than private.

How we achieve intimacy depends a lot on our cultural expectations and conditioning. In Japan, intimacy is often wordless. When people gather to see the cherry blossom in spring, they do not provide a running commentary on how beautiful it is. Nonetheless, they watch it as a shared experience, not a private one. In the West, with its emphasis on *logos*, intimacy is achieved primarily by talking. This is another reason why the apparently diametric differences between tearooms and cafés disguise a potentially deeper connection. The tearoom is largely silent, the café is full of chatter, because in both intimacy is being sought.

The best cafés are perhaps those that manage to provide both privacy and intimacy when wanted. They are places both for dignified solitude and civilised discussion. Regular customers can get to know each other and staff, going beyond superficial pleasantries to genuine friendships. At the same time, it is understood that, if people want to read or talk undisturbed, that will be granted to them. This certainly sounds like the ideal café, and if such a thing is rarely found it is perhaps because the kind of intimacy which is second nature in some parts of the world is hard to come by in many Western cities where populations are transient and lives increasingly atomised. Yet it is surely desired. The promise of intimacy is part of the romance of the café. In our imaginations the ideal café is always a kind of second home, a place to feel cosy, to belong, and belonging without intimacy is an impossibility.

If we are looking for the ideal café, we could do worse than look for inspiration from the ideal tearoom. Okakura described the tearoom as an abode of Fancy, Vacancy and the Unsymmetrical. At first glance, these characteristics seems distant from the modern café, but a second look suggests the gap may be closed.

A tearoom is an abode of Fancy because it is 'an ephemeral structure built to house a poetic impulse', a simple hut of wood and bamboo not intended to last. The relevance of this to a culture where buildings are made of stone and brick and often last for centuries may not be obvious, but a café is also an abode of Fancy in important respects. Although its structure may be enduring, everything inside it is ephemeral. In the best cafés this is emphasised by the freshness of any food available and especially of the roasted coffee beans. In supermarkets, packets of coffee have 'best before' dates stretching months into the future. Specialist coffee roasters suggest that coffee begins to lose some of its flavour profile only a few weeks after roasting. A café is therefore rightly seen as a temple to the ephemeral. Without a constant turnover of coffee, cakes and customers, the most palatial of coffeehouses would soon become a site of decay. Perhaps that is why newspapers and magazines are more at home in cafés than books. They too belong to today, and tomorrow are only good for wrapping used coffee grounds.

An abode of Fancy is not only characterised by its ephemerality. For Okakura, the essence of the element of fancy is that the tearoom is 'created to meet some individual artistic requirement. The tearoom is made for the tea master, not the tea-master for the tearoom.' This spirit of fancy is found in individual cafés of character all over the world, decorated rather than built according to the idiosyncratic tastes of the proprietor. Owners who are true disciples of Coffeeism are driven to open their own cafés because they have some kind of vision of how a café should be that that they have not found fully embodied elsewhere. This starts with the coffee, where every barista has a personal view on the ideal machinery, bean, roast, grind, milk (or the forbidding of milk), crockery and cutlery to deliver the perfect drink. It extends to the environment, the kind of decoration, the lighting, the music or silence, what reading matter, if any, is provided.

Devotees of Coffeeism recognise this fancy when they see it, and can also sniff out its ersatz imitations. Professional interior designers try to create it by following the 'shabby-chic' playbook, as though any old reclaimed furniture and interior decoration would do. Chains struggle most with this. They build their brands on uniformity, but affection is built on individuality. That is why they have struggled to achieve dominance in countries where coffee drinking has a deep-rooted history and where the small owner-run independents offer both quality and value.

Until recently, however, in the Anglo-Saxon world uniformity has been a powerful strategy since it offered a reliability of quality which could sadly not be guaranteed by the old-fashioned coffee shops the chains displaced. Now more and more independents are opening up and the chains are having to rethink. Some are trying to make individual branches more distinctive; others are abandoning the national branding altogether and masquerade as independents. Their challenge could not be put more clearly than the question: how can we make our cafés abodes of Fancy?

How to make them abodes of Vacancy seems even more difficult, since this refers to the tearoom's almost complete lack of ornamentation 'except for what may be placed in it to satisfy some aesthetic need of the moment'. This is sure to evoke an image of austere, angular minimalism, a far cry from the warmth and soft surfaces of the ideal café.

To understand how Vacancy can still be a characteristic of a Western-style café, it is important first to note that there is nothing cold or austere about the Japanese style. Western minimalism is not Japanese minimalism. Western minimalism has its roots in the asceticism of Protestant puritanism, where any excess is a sin. Japanese minimalism has no such moralistic basis. The aesthetic precedes the ethical. Its concern is to make a space clear enough for persons to occupy it with perfect harmony, the body completing the room's contents rather than competing with them. Such an environment is warm, not cold, because it invites you in to take your place in it. In contrast, the feeling evoked by many Western minimalist interiors is that one dare not enter for fear of upsetting their pristine purity.

Vacancy is not therefore primarily a matter of physical emptiness, but of leaving vacant a space in the room for the visitor to fill with comfort. This is exactly what is required of an ideal café. It must feel as though there is a table, a chair, that is waiting for you to occupy. For this, a certain absence of clutter and presence of cleanliness is required. A table that still has the empty cups of long-left guests, or even worse, their crumbs and smears, cries to be given a wide berth, not to be occupied. An excess of menus or condiments also claims too much possession of the space: they should be easily available but not commanding your attention. Nor should the tables and chairs be too uniform in shape or arrangement. There should be a sense that among them are some better suited to you than others. Uniformity suggests that each guest must accommodate herself to the space, not that the space is designed to accommodate her.

More subtly, a café must not suggest that its customers ought to conform to a certain social type. If it is a place for connoisseurs, it should not advertise the fact too much so that those less schooled in coffee feel ignorant in comparison. If it is proud to be independent, it should temper its pride or else it will undo its individuality by declaring its allegiance to the tribe of independents, a tribe not all visitors will identify with. A café should be at ease with itself so its customers can be at ease with themselves, sufficiently secure in its own skin not to have to shout its identity.

Such an abode of Vacancy will naturally also be an abode of the Unsymmetrical, 'consecrated to the worship of the Imperfect, purposely leaving some thing unfinished for the play of the imagination to complete'. The sense of incompletion is one that suggests the customers themselves are required to complete it; the sense of imperfection is, in turn, just this sense that it is incomplete. Physical asymmetry is important to achieve this effect. Perfect physical symmetry can only be spoiled by anyone entering the scene and thereby unsettling the balance. That is why no one's image of the ideal café involves lines of uniformly arranged tables.

For all its differences from a tearoom, a café can also be an abode of Fancy, Vacancy and the Unsymmetrical, and so also 'a

A café should be at ease with itself
so its customers can be at ease
with themselves.

sanctuary from the vexations of the outer world'. Even samurai when entering the tearoom would leave their swords outside. This was like leaving a part of them behind, a part of them that was deeply tied to the struggle and violence of the wider world.

Sadly, there are still parts of the world where the custom of leaving a weapon outside a café would be welcome. For most, however, perhaps there is something else that should be at least disarmed when we enter the sanctuary: our smartphones. There are already some cafés that prohibit their use, but not many. Even these tend to ban only talking on them rather than staring at them. Hence the pitiable sight in so many of our cafés of people fixated by the pocket computers in their hands, even when they are in pairs or groups. The paradox is that almost everyone considers this a lamentable state of affairs but almost everyone contributes to creating it. Our phones seem to demand that we check them, and we seem helpless to resist their call.

To lament the worship of the mobile risks seeming fogeyish and out of time. But unless we think what is of the now is always best, sometimes even the least nostalgic have to admit that what is out of date is often preferable to what is up to date. The fixation with the small screen interferes with too much of what is good about the café. Instead of enjoying either serene solitude or true social engagement, we instead enter a restless state of interaction without real connection, communication without contact, neither fully here nor elsewhere.

We have become so attached to our phones that we often feel incomplete without them. But then so were the swords of the samurai intimately tied to their identities. They nonetheless realised that there are times when we even have to put parts of ourselves to one side. We could and should do the same.

If we are to banish phones from our cafés, should we also insist that the ubiquitous provision of free wi-fi should also be turned on its head, so that cafés boast about being internet-free zones? For many, that would seem a step too far. The café is often a place of work or study, or somewhere to stop and plan the rest of the day's travels, or to write to our friends and relatives back home. Such activities used to involve books, paper and postcards, and we cannot pretend that now they don't more often involve entering cyberspace. Why deny customers the ability to do with modern media what they used to do with the old? It is also true that we have a different relationship to our laptops or tablets than we do to our phones. We are more in charge of when we open them, and more able to turn them off and put them away. Whereas our phones follow us into cafés, computers only join us if we choose to take them out of our bags.

Still, there is something special about those cafés that don't provide wi-fi. Even if you think you are going to get your laptop out, discovering there is no internet can feel like a liberation. It is not your fault you can't work, so you may as well just enjoy the respite enforced insulation brings. There is a special joy in finding yourself in a sanctuary from the vexations of the outer world when you didn't realise you were entering one.

# V
# The Schools of Coffee

Talk of coffee disguises the fact that we live in a world of many coffees. An Italian arriving in 1970s Britain would certainly not have recognised the long, muddy instant beverage commonly served under the same name as his beloved espresso. As the coffee culture grows today, a comic scene is often played out where an elderly customer asks for a coffee, only to be offered a range of choices. Baffled, he replies, 'Just an ordinary coffee,' oblivious to the fact that what counts as 'ordinary' is highly contingent on time and place.

Coffee hasn't even always been a drink. Today, an Ethiopian people called the Oromo maintain an earlier tradition of eating a compressed mass of animal fat and macerated coffee cherries. I have not had the pleasure of trying it, but I suspect there is probably a good reason why this did not conquer the world as the liquid version did.

The earliest ways of brewing the coffee are similar to those still used in Turkey and parts of the Middle East today. Ground coffee is simply heated with water in a pot, usually with sugar, and the liquid is then poured into a cup, leaving as many of the grounds behind in the pot as possible. Done skilfully, this crude method can produce an extremely pleasant, dark, slightly viscous brew. The addition of spices such as anise, cinnamon sticks, cardamon, cloves or nutmeg to the pot also adds layers of flavour absent from more so-called advanced methods, and is certainly preferable to the sprinkling of ground cinnamon or the addition of flavoured syrups.

Turkish coffee reflects the ambiguity of our attitudes towards the 'primitive'. On the one hand, it retains an unpretentious innocence that more developed versions have lost. It maintains a closer link between fruit and drink, the traces of ground coffee not so much a sign of an unrefined imperfection but a visceral reminder of the connection of the drink with the earth. On the other hand, to choose to this way of making coffee when we have acquired so many better methods would seem to be a perverse rejection of the superior for the 'authentic'.

Why then have some cultures held on to the method? The truth is that, where there is a choice, few do hang on to it. In Athens, locals are less likely to ask for *éna ellinikó kafé* (a Greek coffee) than a *frappé* – an iced, milky, foamy instant coffee. Still, a certain attachment to the old ways persist, with good reason. Food and drink do not just exist as discrete items on a menu, to be selected purely for their own intrinsic merits. They are embedded in culture and history. Our culinary preferences form part of our identities, largely because our identities are formed by culture and history.

If we were to act entirely like professional tasters, instantly jettisoning foods and drinks when something better – from a neutral, objective viewpoint – came along, we would be alienating ourselves from part of who we are, and the people and places that made us. The modern cosmopolitan, therefore, is constantly engaged in a balancing act, not so attached to her own culture to avoid experiencing the best of others, but not so promiscuous as to lose contact with home. The old Turkish-style coffee pot persists where it has roots, even if most of the coffee drunk comes from a different vessel.

Humans have always been in pursuit of the highest beauty our humble earth can produce, and so we have used our ingenuity to try to improve on this elemental version. The most basic realisation was that boiling makes the coffee bitter and destroys many of the complexities of its flavour. Although it is possible to apply this insight using the Turkish method, it is difficult to keep the heat under precise control. A French development, however, made it easier. The coffee was placed in a linen bag and infused in hot, but not boiling, water. This not only enabled a clean separation of drink and grounds, but also produced a smoother, less bitter brew.

This method, however, introduced a controversy that poses a constant threat of schism to the more fundamentalist followers of Coffeeism. Cloth and paper filters of any kind hold back most of the oils produced by brewing coffee. For some, this is a gain, since these produce much of the acidity and bitterness that many do not like in coffee. (It has the additional benefit of removing cafestol, a compound found only in the oily fraction of coffee which has been shown to significantly raise levels of 'bad' LDL cholesterol levels.) However, others insist that these oils carry with them some of the distinctive flavours and that to remove them reduces the complexity of the finished drink.

Incredibly, some believe that this difference of opinion is not ultimately to be resolved on the basis of personal preference but on fact and truth. Yet both sides agree completely on what happens. They differ only on what they think the most desirable option of the two is. The school that tends to be most dogmatic here is the one that insists that retaining the oils is essential to retaining the full flavour profile of the coffee.

But this would only be automatically a good thing if maximising the number of flavour variables was the ultimate goal of gastronomy. Obviously it is not. Cooking and brewing aim to achieve the most perfect harmony and balance between the flavours involved. Sometimes this requires the suppression or elimination of flavours that unsettle the balance: a little sugar might be added to a tomato sauce to reduce its acidity, for example.

That is also why it is too dogmatic to insist, as some do, that coffee is only fresh for two weeks after roasting. A roasted coffee bean changes as it ages, and although overall this can be characterised in terms of loss, its optimal age from the point of view of perfect balance might be later in the stage of decay. Each coffee is different, and to insist that fresher is always better is simply wrong. Most roasters say that coffee should not be used within a day or two after roasting because when it is too fresh it is still releasing gases which give the coffee a slightly metallic taste – a perfect example of how losing a flavour can be a good thing.

Each cup of coffee is a unique blend of the variety of bean, the particular harvest, how it was roasted, how it was brewed, the water used to make it, the cup it is served in, the work of the barista, even the atmospheric and lighting conditions, all of which we know alter how we experience taste. All of this leaves out the vital component without which there is no drink as such but merely an amount of flavoured water: the drinker. The coffee has its qualities and so does the drinker, and each time the two come together something unique is created. The perfect cup of coffee cannot be one that is undrunk, and so perfection can never be attributed to the drink alone, only the state produced when it meets its drinker.

The debate about flavour profile is most evidently empty when it comes to darkness of roast. Many coffee snobs insist that dark roasts are for the ignorant, since the darker the roast, the more the flavours produced by roasting occlude those of the bean itself. This argument has two fatal flaws. First, it assumes that flavours produced by roasting are somehow less authentic than those already evident in the bean. But, clearly, roasting adds flavours as well as taking them away, and there is no objective reason to prefer those lost over those gained.

Second, most accept that espresso coffee requires a darker roast, which means to be consistent light-roast fundamentalists should maintain the absurdity that a whole category of coffee is based on defective beans.

What this scholastic debate really shows is that rigid dogmatism has no place in Coffeeism. Celebrating the messy, organic,

The coffee has its qualities
and so does the drinker,
and each time the two come together
something unique is created.

dynamic nature of life, Coffeeism is utterly opposed to all attempts to reduce the chaos of the world to neat formulas. There can be no algorithm for the perfect coffee, just as there can be no algorithm for the perfect life.

Pure romantic poppycock, the cynics cry. Excellence in coffee has been achieved precisely by attending to science and precision. To make an espresso, it is specified that 7–9g of coffee should be finely ground, tamped with 30–40lb of pressure in the portafilter, extracted by 1oz of water at 90.5–93.3 °C (195–200 °F) and 8–10 bars pressure for 28–30 seconds. That is, unless you believe another authority which specifies a more elastic 5–9g of coffee, 25–40lb of tamp pressure, 1–1¼oz of water at 85–95 °C (185–201 °F) at 7–11 bars pressure for 20–30 seconds. These differences of opinion are small, but the fact that they exist at all shows the absurdity of specifying the exact variables with such precision.

Historically, the baristas who made the great espressos that eventually took over the world never got out their scales or measures. Yes, they made sure their machines were calibrated correctly for temperature and pressure but they made adjustments when they could see and smell the coffee coming out differently, not when they observed a dial had moved. Through long practice, making thousands of drinks, they developed the practical wisdom to be able to use their own personal judgement, an instrument far more subtle than any thermometer or pressure gauge. The reason for this is simple: the number of variables that affect how a coffee turns out is not exhausted by the checklist provided by standard 'recipes'. Factors such as the environmental air pressure and humidity in the room, the exact nature of each roast and slight differences in water mineral content can all make a difference. The master coffee maker may not know exactly what is different but she will observe the result and adjust accordingly.

The reliance on rules and measures emerged in a culture that came to fetishise science and mistrust human judgement. Perhaps more importantly, it was a way of providing a short cut for novices, so that they could make very good coffee very quickly, without the expense and investment of a long apprenticeship. With a weekend course and half a dozen simple rules to follow, anyone could be made a respectable barista. The problem is that, when you learn that way, all can become adequate but none can become excellent.

In the modern world, however, the alternative is just too demanding. Tokyo has more Michelin-starred restaurants than any other city in the world. The secret of its pre-eminence is the Japanese culture of apprenticeship at the feet of the *shokunin*, the master artisan. To become a great sushi chef, for example, you might first have to spend years simply mastering the art of cooking rice or making *tamago*, an egg sushi. No doubt there are already machines, probably made in Japan, that can cook the sushi rice well enough to pass muster with all but the most refined of gourmands. But put your commis in charge of that and she will never be able to surpass it.

Yes, but the optimistic technophile will still say, what if we could mechanise and formalise the process so that it really could match the very best? Will anything other than romanticism stop you conceding defeat when a capsule machine wins the world barista award? No. Romanticism will indeed be what stands between us and accepting the dominance of algorithms and machines, because romance is an essential part of coffee, as a culinary experience. The production of coffee is not just a process; it is an exchange, an interaction, in which the barista puts part of herself into a cup and invites you to share it.

Of course, the microscope does not detect anything missing in the coffee that emerges after you press a button as opposed to one that comes from a human hand. But we are not looking for molecules or occult ingredients. What we are looking for is a relation between people, beans and water. Such relations are not like magnetic fields, detectable by scientific equipment, but they are real and anyone who ignores them ignores a large part of what it is to be human.

Coffeeism's veneration for the artisan should not in any way be mistaken for an anti-scientism. The development of coffee making owes a great deal to the ingenuity of culinary engineers and the insights of gastronomic science. Take, for example, the vacuum pot, invented in Berlin in the 1830s, with many patented variants following in its wake. This ingenious, albeit rather cumbersome device produced such good coffee that it remained popular well into the twentieth century. Many Americans, for

The production of coffee is not just
a process; it is an exchange,
an interaction, in which the barista
puts part of herself into a cup
and invites you to share it.

example, still remember the Silex coffee filter, first made in the 1910s with recently invented heat-resistant Pyrex.

A vacuum pot comprises two glass globes, fixed together in an egg-timer arrangement with a siphon connecting them. A filter and coffee are placed in the upper chamber, water in the lower. As the lower chamber is heated, the air pressure increases, pushing water up through the siphon into the upper chamber where it mixes with the coffee grounds. The Italian metal moka pot, popularised by the Milanese engineer Alfonso Bialetti (1888–1970) in 1933, exploits the same basic principle, but the liquid remains in the upper chamber and the grounds are kept separate in a third, intermediate well. In a vacuum pot, however, after enough time for the coffee to brew but not so much that it turns bitter, the heat is removed and, as the lower chamber cools, a partial vacuum is created, pulling the liquid from the top chamber back into the lower.

Perhaps the greatest single technological leap in the making of coffee was the introduction of high-pressure espresso machines to extract more from the ground coffee than is possible by previous methods. The first of these was patented in 1884 by Angelo Moriondo (1851–1914) of Turin. One of the initial attractions of this had nothing to do with the taste but the speed of preparation, hence the name *espresso*. Early versions, however, were tricky to use and often produced very bitter coffee because they relied on boiling water and steam. In 1947 Giovanni Achille Gaggia (1895–1961), a Milanese café owner, created a system that used a spring-loaded, lever-operated piston which used a higher pressure but cooler water. This gave birth to a whole new element of coffee: the golden *crema* that crowns a true espresso. Only coffee extracted at high pressure is able to emulsify the oils in the drink to create what, after some initial suspicion, was quickly embraced as the hallmark of a quality coffee.

Each step forward in the development of coffee making expresses values associated with their epochs. For the first Arab drinkers, what was needed was a simple, portable method for making a drink used to keep them awake and alert. When coffee came to Europe, just as the Renaissance was reaching its peak, first to Venice in 1615 and then quickly sweeping the continent, drinkers sought more refinement through filtering. Vacuum pots reflected the Victorian fascination with science and technology as well as the new interest in elaborate domestic devices that impressed with their modernity and theatricality. As the Industrial Revolution progressed, speed and efficiency became key desiderata, and the espresso came to dominate.

Today, the growing technology is the fully mechanised capsule system. These expensive machines and their expensive pods are not only coming to more and more homes, but are also increasingly used in the catering trade. They are even found in Michelin-starred restaurants, since dedicated baristas would be idle most of the time and the machines perform better than waiters. We need not fear their total domination, however, since their rise coincides with the elevation of the art of the barista. This make sense: the more we appreciate the skill of the real barista, the more we accept that it is futile to think we can do anywhere near as well at home, and so we give in and let technology do it for us.

However, there is an alternative to the wastefulness and extravagance of capsule systems: simple filtering. For those willing to make a little more effort, a cheap invention called the AeroPress has been impressing coffee connoisseurs. Requiring no electricity, this simple device combines the virtues of steeping and filtering with the added extraction power of air pressure, created by no more than the manual depression of a sealed plunger. In an age where the solutions we are offered so often involve expensive technology, it is heartening to see an innovation which returns coffee to its simpler essence and retains the human touch in its preparation.

# vi
# Aesthetic Appreciation

Coffeeism, like Teaism, is a 'religion of aestheticism' to use Okakura's phrase. It worships the immanent, visible beauty of the world, not the transcendent, invisible majesty of the heavens. This veneration is different from that of Western aesthetes, who seek refined beauty and dismiss the ordinary. Books on aesthetics deal almost exclusively with the visual, literary, theatrical and musical arts. Space is sometimes granted to natural beauty, but there is little to nothing said about the aesthetics of daily life, especially food and drink. Restaurant critics are simply not in the same category as art critics. Food and drink pages of newspapers and magazines are found in 'lifestyle' sections, not the art pages.

Of course, it is easily granted that there is an aesthetic dimension to food, but to dignify it with the same seriousness as art is considered vulgar and ridiculous. Western aesthetics becomes elitist, in contrast to Teaism's 'spirit of Eastern democracy' which makes 'all its votaries aristocrats in taste'. What sad lives we would lead if we truly believed in this gulf between high art and quotidian beauty. Most of us spend a small fraction of our time in art galleries, theatres or concert halls, and less time than we would wish reading great literature or watching art movies. Are we then condemned to live largely alienated from great beauty, only able to contemplate it on those occasions where we are specifically engaged with art?

Coffeeism suggests a more hopeful alternative. It alerts us to the possibility that beauty surrounds us, that any absence of aesthetic appreciation is due more to our own inattention than to the absence of anything worthy of it. Our daily ritual of sitting with our coffee and drinking it mindfully is a kind of meditative practice for a wider mindfulness of the countless other moments of beauty that can easily escape our notice when we are drifting through life.

It takes some readjustment to truly see this. Take, for example, the sight of a beautiful sunset above the horizon juxtaposed with an ugly, busy urban ring road beneath it. We are apt to think that such a sunset is wasted on its location, that it belongs opposite a tranquil beach or at the end of an Alpine valley. Yet in another sense there is no more fitting place to appreciate the

Coffeeism alerts us to the possibility
that beauty surrounds us,
that any absence of aesthetic
appreciation is due more to our own
inattention than to the absence
of anything worthy of it.

We need the bitter to bring out the sweet, a culinary metaphor that will ring true to all coffeeistas.

remarkable capacity of the world to provide brief moments of utter delight in even the most unpromising of settings. Amid the ugly, the beautiful stands out even more, reminding us of just how precious it is.

Our problem is that we want our beauty untainted. We seek it as an escape from the ugliness of life when we should see it as a way of helping us to tolerate it. Rather than offering us respite from our trials, beauty should help us through them. Art and beauty are palliative, not curative.

The cultivation of aesthetic attention and appreciation should focus our minds on the way the world is or could realistically be, not on as it is not and could never be. One central focus of this attention is *mono no aware*, a bittersweet appreciation of the fundamental sadness of the impermanence of all life. When we feel the 'pathos of things' we feel them more deeply. It is only when we truly appreciate how wonderful things are that we can profoundly feel the sadness of their transience. We need the bitter to bring out the sweet, a culinary metaphor that will ring true to all coffeeistas. Coffee's bitterness means it is not a drink for children.

Bitterness has no virtue in itself, of course. The history of brewing methods is in part the quest to reduce it. What the coffeeista understands, however, is that without any bitter notes at all, coffee is not coffee. In its wholeness, it needs its yin and yang.

It is also precisely this bitterness that makes coffee the perfect accompaniment for the sweet. Whether it's an Italian dunking a hard almond *cantuccino* into an espresso, a German enjoying afternoon *Kaffee und Kuchen*, Swedes sharing a *fika* with cinnamon buns, a Canadian with a filter coffee and a muffin, everyone knows the special pleasure of matching coffee with a sweet treat.

For the true coffeista, however, this is a genuine matching, not the kind of suffocation of the bitter by sucrose. Or, for that matter, by lactose: there are long lattes and cappuccinos which are better described as hot milky drinks with a hint of coffee, especially when a flavoured syrup or topping is added. Add to these all the tiny cups of espresso to which so much sugar is added that the drink is barely liquid, and it would seem that, although coffee has conquered the world, most people don't really like its taste.

It sounds paradoxical, but it is true. A senior executive at a coffee company once confided to me that, if they asked their customers what kind of coffee they preferred, they would say, 'Dark, rich and strong.' In blind tastings, however, they preferred lighter, weaker brews. And, of course, what they choose to drink is in any case usually highly diluted with milk, heavily sweetened, or both.

It might seem odd that we are such bad judges of our own tastes, but in fact there is often a mismatch between what we think we are going to enjoy and how much we actually enjoy it. This is partly because of smell. Many find the odour of cheese

unpleasant, but love eating it. In contrast, they find the smell of coffee irresistible but find drinking it a disappointment. These are extreme examples, but anticipated pleasure rarely perfectly matches actual pleasure. (Chocolate is one of the few foods where it does.)

But why then do people not learn to distrust their noses? Because the nose is correct and what we call flavour is largely olfactory anyway. The tongue picks up on only a small rage of tastes: sweet, sour, bitter, salty and umami. Some scientists make the case for various candidates as a sixth, and India's Ayurvedic tradition does list six tastes: Sweet, Sour, Salty, Bitter, Pungent and Astringent. However you categorise taste, it is well understood that most of what we call 'flavours' are smells detected by the nose, not tastes perceived by the tongue.

What happens when we drink coffee is that the nose and the tongue are forced to confront their disagreements. The nose still likes what it smells, but the tongue is more ambivalent, if not totally hostile. For a minority, this combination of flat and sharp creates a harmonious chord; for others, the result is a dissonance that they seek to correct by adding other, sweeter notes.

The fact that many do not like the taste of coffee in no way negates the evident truth that many people like coffee very much indeed. It only reinforces the basic premise of Coffeeism: that coffee is about much more than its flavour. People are attracted by what coffee promises them, which in Okakura's phrase is 'the utmost beatitude of the mundane'. People who drink coffee only when its primary flavours are significantly masked are not so much in denial of their true desires as seeking satisfaction of desires much more profound than the simple wish for pleasant food and drink.

No matter how much one likes or dislikes coffee, everyone is capable of appreciating it. Unfortunately, in a world in which everyone has been told that their own preferences are sovereign and that all they need to do is satisfy them, the distinctions between liking and appreciating, the pleasant and the good, have been lost. Without such distinctions, however, proper aesthetic appreciation of any kind is impossible. There would be nothing more to say in an art gallery or after a performance of an opera than 'I liked it' or 'I didn't like it'.

When we attend more carefully to any aesthetic object, we notice that it has real qualities, whether we personally like them or not. You may not like Mozart, but if you cannot see that he is a greater genius than Salieri, you have not been using your ears. You may think there is something childlike in some of Picasso's Cubist works, but if you really think a child could have painted them you have not been using your eyes. You may not like the floral and fruity flavour of an expertly prepared cup of Ethiopian Yirgacheffe, but if you cannot tell that it is a superior quality to a cup of instant coffee, you haven't been using your nose and tongue.

Aesthetic appreciation requires us to look beyond what we like and don't like, and to perceive the real qualities in the thing itself. This simple truth is almost a heresy in a world in which *De gustibus non set disputandum* (There is no disputing taste) has become a democratic rallying cry, especially when it comes to food and drink. Surely, there is nothing more to be said about taste than how it tastes to me. Taste is subjective, not objective.

The sincerity of this belief is called into question by the haste with which people are apt to insist to friends 'Taste this!' when they stumble on something delightful. Of course, all our tastes are different, but we also assume, correctly, that most of what we can detect in a drink, others can, too. Either this as a remarkably improbable coincidence, or it is explained by the simple fact that what we detect is really there. Unless I have a very strange palate, if I have chosen my words carefully and say that my Fazenda IP Brazilian coffee has notes of cocoa and hazelnut, those flavours are in a real sense in the coffee, not just in my perception of it.

When people first truly attend to the coffee they have been absentmindedly drinking for a lifetime and notice the variety and depth of flavours it contains, it can be a moment of real epiphany. The door opens to a whole new world of experience. In their haste to understand it, some try to educate themselves in the esoteric language of tasters, studying the coffee flavour wheel and trying to apply this new knowledge. The wheel provides a kind of map for making sense of this new terrain. They learn to note a coffee's body, its acidity, its darkness of roast. They distinguish between the broad categories of flavour such as fruit, floral, chocolate, nut, sweet and spice. Then they turn to the more specific subdivisions such as lime, grapefruit, raisin, caramel, hazelnut, black pepper, lavender.

The wheel is a useful tool, but too often coffeeistas fail to appreciate the insight common to both Zen and Taoism that our language and concepts cannot capture the richness of experience, but can only gesture towards it, like a finger pointing at the moon. We can use words to get us close to the thing itself, but to touch it we have to leave words behind. Such is the function of the flavour wheel. Its use is to help train us to attend to the flavours in the coffee. But once we start to become skilled at this, our concepts become obstacles, not accessories, to ever finer perception. There are more flavours in coffee than can captured in a finite list, more than the six

When people first truly
attend to the coffee they have been
absentmindedly drinking
for a lifetime, it can be a moment
of real epiphany.

which roughly correspond to the flavours of berries, or the seven forms of citrus.

The ultimate goal is not to be able to identify and label the distinct flavours in a coffee but to appreciate it in its fullness, richness and wholeness, without the need to apply categories. First, we think that coffee just tastes like coffee. Then we notice this taste is reminiscent of caramel and mandarin, with low acidity and medium body. Finally, we think that each coffee just tastes like the coffee it is, only now we really know what coffee tastes like.

Something remarkable happens when we are able to attend to our aesthetic experiences and see beyond our preferences to the way things are. What is in one sense purely subjective becomes objective, the inner becomes outer, the private becomes shared. The world exists only phenomenologically, and yet incredibly we can enter a shared phenomenological space with others. This possibility is denied us when we insist that there is nothing to aesthetic appreciation than our own perceptions. Aesthetic appreciation, too often assumed to be the most personal thing in the world, is what enables us to most deeply escape solipsism and share the world with others.

# vii
# Coffee Masters

Tea masters were universally revered and respected in traditional Japanese society. Today's Western coffee masters – baristas and roasters – are widely ridiculed and denigrated: beardy, nerdy hipsters with an unhealthy obsession, making a killing by charging gullible foodies extortionate prices for what is, after all, just coffee. In a world where some monks are scoundrels and priest tyrants, it would be foolish to pretend baristas are all secular saints. But could the antipathy towards them reflect the fact that they make many of us uncomfortable in ways we cannot quite put our finger on?

First and foremost, they represent a kind of expertise that we do not understand. Expertise in general is more and more distrusted, but at least with doctors, engineers, architects we know what it is that they know that we don't. To acknowledge the expertise of a coffee master is to admit that we don't know a great deal about something we took to be entirely democratic and unmysterious. They rob us of our innocent assumption that, as long as we know what we like, we know all we need to know. To admit their superior knowledge is to humble ourselves, and if there is one thing the modern world is not good at, it's humility.

Second, these experts are often so young, so apparently care-free. We are used to authorities who are more sombre, more respectable-looking, more senior. To defer to people who look like they belong on skateboards is unsettling.

Finally, when we are so often struggling to find meaning and purpose, it is a kind of affront to see people finding fulfilment in something so mundane as coffee. Why have philosophers and sages puzzled over the meaning of life for centuries if the answer is to be found in a hot infusion?

We need to turn these sources of suspicion into reasons for admiration. We should study at the feet of these masters to see how it is possible for the simplest of things to be full of mystery and complexity, for meaning to be found in the mundane. Nor do we have to wait until we are grey to have the wisdom to live well. Wisdom is a journey, and although age can take us further along its road, it is never too soon to start out. In any case, since it is a journey without end, what matters most is to be travelling, not what stage we have reached.

The ideal (perhaps idealised) roaster or barista shows that *satori* (enlightenment) can indeed be find in a coffee cup. If this sounds absurd, it is because we tend to think of *satori* as an exceptional state, the culmination of a journey of a lifetime, if not several. However, there are many precedents

for the idea that enlightenment is something available in the here and now. Jōdo Shinshū or Shin Buddhism, the form of Pure Land Buddhism that is dominant in Japan, teaches that enlightenment cannot be attained by our own efforts. All we need to do is give ourselves over to the 'other power' by reciting the name of Amitābha Buddha. For this reason it is known as the 'easy path', in contrast to the hard path of Zen. Clearly, however, followers who do this are not transformed into exceptional beings, their purity evident to all. *Satori* is a much more everyday state that we go in and out of.

Even those who follow the hard path of Zen often talk in ways which suggest enlightenment leaves the world very much as it was. There is a Zen proverb, 'Before Enlightenment, chop wood, carry water. After Enlightenment, chop wood, carry water.' Something changes, for sure, but that something is subtle, inner, barely perceptible to the outside.

A certain deflation of the idea of enlightenment is in any case in order, even if the *satori* of the coffee master is not on a par with that of the Zen master. We live in a disenchanted world in which the promise of something higher and purer rings increasingly hollow. Teaism took steps towards a more immanent religiosity and Coffeeism should complete the journey. *Satori* today is the realisation that this world is all there is, our experience is all we know of it, and that the only unchanging truth is that everything is always changing.

It is no surprise that the true coffee master should have achieved this enlightenment, and tries to maintain it by her discipline. Every day she devotes herself to making the most of what she is now making or drinking, fully accepting its transience and her own. This is not a passive resignation to her own mortality but an active encounter with it. It requires a recognition that we can see the beauty and wonder in the everyday only if we make ourselves worthy of it by granting all our tasks and activities the attention they deserve.

The coffee drinker must cultivate a similar attitude, making ourselves worthy of receiving what the barista makes for us by giving it the respect of our full attention. At its best, therefore, the serving of coffee enables what Okakura calls a 'sympathetic communion of minds' in which the spirit of the barista's offering is met in the spirit of the customer's taking.

There is one way in which the barista resembles the traditional depiction of the Buddha. She may look serious when at work, but her life is one of small joys, one that puts a gentle smile on her lips. Stories about Zen masters often portray them laughing uproariously, at least when they are not beating novices. They are

We can see the beauty and
wonder in the everyday only
if we make ourselves worthy of it
by granting all our tasks and activities
the attention they deserve.

lively, puckish fellows, not dull, sanctimonious saints. For what else are we to do when we see this world as it is, and our pathetic place in it? The French Existentialists saw the absurdity of life and furrowed their brows. Comedians see the absurdity of life and life at it. They are more truly philosophers who know what Okakura called 'the noble secret of laughing at yourself, calmly yet thoroughly' wearing 'the smile of philosophy'.

However, the *satori* of the coffee master does not conform to the stereotype of the tranquil Buddha sat in the lotus position, for it is found in ceaseless activity. Yet there is a kind of tranquillity there, a complete absorption in the task which is a kind of meditative state. Westerners often misunderstand the tranquillity of meditation as a kind of deep relaxation, almost sleeping. Nothing could be further from the truth. *Satori* is often described as an awakening, not a falling asleep. In meditation we are more alert, not less. It is no coincidence therefore coffee is a stimulant, not a relaxant. Caffeine sharpens our minds. The good life we seek is not one of dull serenity but acute, wakeful awareness. Coffee can lead us to it, if we have the wisdom to know how to follow its call.

# Afterword

I am aware that, as you reach the end of this book, a growing weight of expectation centres on your next cup of coffee. I want to explore the idea that it might hold within it such intense opportunities and realisations as enlightenment or beauty. I hope that this book has created a mixture of feelings and thoughts within you. Reading Julian's words, I certainly veered between deep agreement and occasional disagreement, but I enjoyed having to wrestle with why I might have disagreed with him and whether my position was fixed or mutable. However, what attracted me most to this book, what made it meaningful to me, was the connection of philosophy to the practical. Every day I make coffee, every day I drink coffee, and so every day (if I choose) I can leverage that linear process of making and consuming into something more. I'd like to explore how you might do that, too.

I am not going to pretend for one moment that I have any masterful insights in Zen Buddhism with which to guide you. I would be deeply uncomfortable with calling myself a master artisan, or *shokunin*, within the world of coffee. What I want to share are a few practical moments that we might invest in or use as an opportunity, without compromising the deliciousness of the coffee.

Coffee is a daily ritual for many of us, but that doesn't mean that we have to burden every cup with ceremony. We can pick and choose little moments, when the mood might take us, and we can lean in to how they might make us feel.

What underpins all of this for me is that coffee is so unlikely. It's a gloriously human thing, easily slipping into the absurd when you give it a little thought. The coffee industry will often try to remind people that coffee is a fruit. I disagree. Myriad species across the globe enjoy fruit, for nutrition and for its delightful flavour, distributing its seeds in exchange for sugar. Taking a piece of fruit, squeezing out the seed, discarding the flesh and carefully letting the seed ferment before washing it clean and drying it, then moving it thousands of miles across the globe and placing it in tumbling ovens of immense heat to transform it again, before smashing it tiny pieces, soaking it in hot water and drinking the decoction – that is something only one species could ever do. I love that we have no idea who first looked at those seeds and thought about their potential for transformation through roasting. The window of roasting, where the coffee tastes good, is quite narrow. Who persisted and kept experimenting when their first efforts were probably deeply unpleasant? Who then took this roasted seed and, having found it to taste pretty awful, decided that perhaps they should try smashing it to pieces and boiling it with water? Who, having tasted this deeply bitter drink, ignored the warning signs of a potential poison and kept drinking to the point that they felt the new rush of caffeine through their system?

Every time you open a cupboard and find a jar of coffee inside, you should be shocked. How is this possible? How is this normal? How is this something found in almost every home on the planet? More than this, how do we fail to appreciate that these seeds of a tropical shrub have not cost us a fortune, but are considered such a staple that we might riot if they were taken away?

This is not meant to be a celebration of globalism, of our ability to ignore the human cost of cheap coffee. We cannot be proud of the compromises we have made to keep coffee cheap. I just want to highlight how absurd this situation is, and within that there lies an opportunity.

**The Production of Coffee**
Here's an exercise that you may choose to perform only once, though I don't think it loses its impact when repeated. You can do this when you next weigh the coffee beans for a single cup of coffee. Let's say the dose is 15g. For this dose of coffee, pick two beans at a time from the bag until you have the required weight. This isn't a particularly enjoyable task, and it is finicky and slow. You may count anywhere from 80 to 120 beans in this process. The reason I suggest doing this two beans at a time is because most coffee cherries contain two seeds. If the coffee you are drinking is of speciality grade, then it's likely that this coffee was picked by hand, one cherry at a time. Many varieties of coffee do not ripen uniformly, and so the ripe cherries must be selectively picked. Lower-quality coffee may be stripped from

the branch in a single motion, and in Brazil some coffee may be machine-harvested. The rest is picked cherry by cherry, by nimble and hardworking hands. Think of the time it took you to weigh out the beans for a single cup of coffee, and then think of the global scale of coffee drinking. Think then of the scale of humanity, and then think of the scale of humanity required to produce coffee. It is impossible to grasp, and the exercise of weighing a dose like this should leave one both astonished and uncomfortable.

The scale and scope of coffee is hard to comprehend, not just because of the global logistics involved, with hundreds of thousands of containers shuttling raw coffee across the oceans and continents. The human scale is even harder to wrestle with. You'll constantly hear people in the coffee industry talk about how many hands coffee passes through. They aren't just hands; they're people giving time, skill and expertise to a moment in a coffee bean's journey to you. You'll often see the coffee producer highlighted, but producing coffee is not a singular venture. You should consider that someone may have

spent time sorting the harvested cherries, someone worked a pulper, someone managed the fermentation, several others may have been responsible for drying the coffee. Moving the coffee around, on its way to the dry mill, may involve more people lifting and carrying it, and then someone managing the hulling and many others potentially involved in the sorting – removing individual beans that could make your brew slightly less sweet. All of this before the coffee has even left the country where it was produced, with shipping, roasting, packing and delivery all still to come. Yet we look at the price of a bag of nice coffee and think, 'This is expensive.' There is no blame here – for a long time, a combination of humanity's best and worst qualities combined to keep coffee cheap. Impressive work was done to improve efficiency and make the system better, faster and less wasteful. Yet, at the heart of coffee still lies exploitation. Coffee was brought to many parts of the world because empires saw land and labour they could exploit to make this drink they liked a little cheaper. Today, coffee producers may still end up in a position where they must sell their coffee for less than it cost to grow it.

This is the most complicated part of coffee for me – this juxtaposition between the horrifying past it has not really managed to shake off and the delight in how interesting, how fun, a cup of coffee can be.

**The Ritual of Brewing Coffee**

There is no doubt that there is pleasure and value to be found in the ritual of brewing coffee. There is a pleasing repetition that comes with an understanding of what is happening and what will happen – with just a hint of excitement about the possibility of what might happen. Coffee is a cacophony of variables and, try as we might, true replication of a brew day after day is both tricky and unlikely.

At the heart of modern coffee brewing lies the strange point of disagreement that is a set of weighing scales. This is a somewhat odd sentence to write in the context of coffee and philosophy, but it is a topic that is worth addressing. It allows us to answer the question of what we want from our morning ritual. For some, weighing is antithetical to their desired experience. It is cold, hard science, in opposition to the art or craft of brewing coffee, and it reduces a complex process to one of merely box-ticking. For others, using scales removes distractions, and allows more focus on skills that have been developed or that feel playful in the pursuit of their mastery.

Personally, I don't want to guess what 15g of coffee beans looks like. I don't want to think, as I am pouring water over a bed of coffee, is this 250g of water or is it 260g of water? Undoubtedly, some will say that they can easily discern 'enough' from 'not enough' or 'too much' by sight, but I would argue that, once you've discovered how small changes in a recipe can have a big impact on the taste of a cup of coffee, this is not a game you would wish to play. Especially not before you've had coffee…

Understanding what we enjoy about the ritual allows us to lean into that, and I believe we can reap greater rewards as a result. I don't really, deeply, want to think about the process. I want to

make something, to feel a sense of pride in what I've made, but I also want to lose myself a little bit to the process. Not to the extent that I become like the driver who can't remember a thing about the last 5 miles behind the wheel, but I want to balance focus on the process with being able to turn off the part of my brain that is looking to second-guess what I'm doing.

The point here is not to argue that my way is superior or ideal, but to pick it all apart just a little so that we might understand more about what we enjoy from our morning rituals.

**The Aroma of Coffee**
We've all heard, and probably said, the words 'I love the smell of freshly ground coffee!' Like all clichés, it is rooted in truth, but how much do we really enjoy that smell? When it comes to describing how coffee tastes, many people feel a sense of intimidation or frustration. The world of wine has led us to expect that tasting notes should be florid, with extravagant descriptions of floral and fruity flavours. I meet countless people who feel there is a gap between what they can taste and what the coffee industry tastes. Changing that can start with considering the smell of freshly ground coffee.

Take a moment with the coffee you've just ground. Have a good sniff. It will be heady, charming and perhaps overwhelming. Before we break down those aromas, we have a little housekeeping to do. Your nose, your sense of smell, is an absolute marvel, but it does have a flaw we must consider. When you're smelling your ground coffee, the first sniff will be intense but as you smell again the aroma will seem to fade. As you hunt for a word to describe what you smell, each sniff seems to turn down the volume and those aromas start to feel as though they're drifting from reach. Your experience of a smell is changed by exposure. Your brain will begin to tune out things that appear to be constant, so even though the intensity of the aroma hasn't changed you experience it fading away. This is the mechanism that leads to people who religiously wear the same fragrance every day being completely unaware of just how much they doused themselves with it that morning, in a quest to be able to smell it on themselves again. In a less charming example, it is also why the bathroom doesn't smell bad until you go out and come back in again.

When I want to really pick apart the smell of the coffee grounds, my little hack is to try to reset my sense of smell by using my clothes. Most laundry detergents smell nothing like coffee, and so your clothes are a wonderful contrast. You might feel somewhat absurd sniffing your sleeve or your shoulder, but you'll find that doing so turns back up the aromas of coffee that you're trying to break down.

All of this is a prequel to the opportunity of paying attention to the aroma of coffee. There are many questions you can ask of it, and you can choose which ones you answer. For example, does this remind me of anything? Is it evocative of a day or a place or something else? How is this different from other coffee? What is it that gives this particular aroma its character? What is it that I might recognise if I were to smell this coffee again tomorrow, in among a few others? These questions are far vaguer than the very specific questions that coffee people tend to ask, for example: is this fruity or floral? If it is fruity, then what kind of fruit does it remind me of? Is this fruit ripe, or does it smell as though it has been cooked or processed in some way?

The simplest version of this process is this thought: we describe freshly ground coffee as one of life's great pleasures – are you making sure to enjoy it every day?

**The Taste of Coffee**
There is a famous mindfulness exercise sometimes known as the raisin meditation. It is simple: very slowly eat a single

raisin, paying as much attention to it as you can as you do so. You start with the raisin in your hand, considering its look and its feel. Then you put it in your mouth, paying attention to its sweetness, its texture and how it changes as you chew. Once you swallow the raisin, you consider its journey and how it ended in that moment. This exercise doesn't really require a raisin; any kind of food or drink would be suitable, and I think coffee is a perfect candidate because of the ways in which its flavours evolve rapidly over the course of drinking it.

The first time you try to do this with coffee will be very rewarding. The flavour of great coffees goes through astonishingly large shifts, once you pay attention to it. This evolution of flavour is a mixture of evolving chemistry in the cup, and changes to the way your sense of taste works. If you think about it, you'll probably be aware that temperature really does change the way you perceive things. An ice-cold soft drink is refreshing, but at room temperature it is cloying and unpleasantly sweet. The quantity of sugar in the drink hasn't changed, but your ability to accurately perceive it has. The further something is from body temperature, the less effective we are at tasting it. If you enjoy piping-hot coffee, then sadly there's a chance that you've been missing out. The change isn't just in your own head; small changes are occurring so that the flavour of the coffee evolves over time. When you combine both the change in chemistry and the change in perception, it is delightful and worthy of your undistracted attention. The coffee will seem to open up, flavours that were hard to pick out will become clearer, and – if the coffee is good – it will almost seem to get a little sweeter as it cools, and often a little less bitter, too. You don't have to wait until the coffee is lukewarm, and while many enjoy iced coffee, I am unable to sing the praises of a tepid and room-temperature cup. If you want specificity, the range of 55 °C down to 35 °C (131 °F to 95 °F) is probably the prime tasting window. This is one area where a brewed coffee, like filter coffee, has an advantage over an espresso. You can spend some time with your filter coffee; your enjoyment of an espresso is often fleeting. However, the espresso does offer a longer aftertaste – the lingering flavours on your palate.

If you really want to get more from your cup of coffee, you have to pick it apart a little. For some, this is like unweaving the rainbow – for them, pulling apart a beautiful thing to understand the mechanism behind it destroys the beauty. For many of us, though, there is yet more beauty to be found in the understanding and explanation.

Tasting coffee – in fact, tasting most things – is about picking apart the experience of flavour that your consciousness has gone to great lengths to conjure up as a kind of finished composition. Most of the time when we are listening to music, we're engaged by the lyrics or melody. We're not usually trained to pick apart the mix, to pull out each individual instrument, and consider what it is contributing melodically, rhythmically or sonically. (At this point, you might be starting to consider yourself someone who prefers not to unweave the rainbow, but stay with me.)

Gustation, the experience of tasting, can be broken up into two main elements: taste and flavour. Taste would include the things we experience in the mouth – saltiness, sweetness, bitterness, acidity and umami (savouriness) are the five most commonly discussed. There are other tastes we perceive, such as metallic, astringent or piquant, the heat from spiciness. Alongside those, we also experience the texture of the food or drink, and its temperature.

One of the simplest and most effective ways to develop your sense of taste is to pick one of those key tastes at a time and focus on it. How intense is the acidity in this drink? How much do you like the acidity? Is it refreshing and balanced, or is it sour and dominant? Does it remind you of citrus fruit? Of apples? You may not have answers to more than the first two questions here, but asking them takes you a long way. You can work your way through each of the key tastes and then ask: Is this balanced? Does everything fit together nicely, or is something too loud?

Initially, this can be a slightly frustrating process, but you can accelerate your understanding through comparison. This is admittedly easier with something like wine, but if you're able to brew two different coffees, I strongly recommend comparing them. Asking yourself if one cup is sweeter than another is much easier than trying to assess the sweetness of one cup alone.

## The Appreciation of Coffee

I have one final piece of advice that may seem counterintuitive: once in a while, drink some terrible coffee. If you've developed an interest in coffee, then part of the fun is that every day your coffee tastes great. Without the occasional reminder of how most coffee tastes, I think something of the beauty of excellence is lost. You need a little ugliness to experience beauty, and to appreciate just how beautiful something is.

—**James Hoffmann**

It is not that we should ignore
the claims of posterity,
but that we should seek
to enjoy the present more.

—Kakuzō Okakura, *The Book of Tea* (1906)

# Index

## A
acidity 166
AeroPress 123
aestheticism 75, 124–39
Amitābha Buddha 146
appreciation of coffee 167
aroma of coffee 134, 160–2
Avicenna, *Canon of Medicine* 67–8

## B
baristas 54–9, 98, 113, 123, 143, 145, 147
    skill of brewing coffee 116–19
beans, coffee 81, 113, 154
Beauvoir, Simone de 84
Berkeley, George 48
Bialetti, Alfonso 121
bitterness 131–2
Bodhidharma 62
brewing coffee 110–13, 116–23, 131, 132–3, 158–60
    the first cup of coffee myth 60–2, 64, 153
    rituals of coffee making 13–14, 16, 18, 34
bubonic plague 68
Buddha 146, 147, 149
*buncham* 67
byproducts 82

## C
cafés 84, 88–105
cafestol 112
caffeine 8, 15, 81, 149, 153
cancer 68, 82
cappuccinos 132
capsule system 123
Chan Buddhism 62
Charles II, King 65
Christianity 26, 29–31, 64
Clement VIII, Pope 64
*Coffea arabica* 80
coffee culture 28–9, 79, 109
coffee masters 140–9
coffee mornings 64
coffee pots, Turkish-style 111
coffeehouses 15, 64–5, 77, 79, 84, 91
Coffeeism 32–8, 41, 59, 62–4, 87, 114, 116
    aesthetic appreciation 128
    basic premise of 28–9, 135
    link to Teaism 28, 29, 81
    true devotees of 68, 70–1, 98
    veneration of the artisan 119
    Zen and Taoist roots of 45
conformity 53, 54
connections 84
cost 153–4, 157
*crema* 122

## D
*de gustibus non set disputandum* 136
dementia 68
Dōgen, *Instructions to the Zen Cook* 70
drinkers 114, 122, 147
Dufour, Philippe Sylvestre 67

## E

eavesdropping 92, 93
enlightenment 145–7, 149
espresso machines 121–2
espressos 79–80, 109, 114, 116–17, 122, 132, 165
experience 49–50, 51, 52, 86
expertise 143–4

## F

Fancy, abodes of 96–9, 101–3
filter coffee 164–5
filters 112, 121, 123
flavour 97, 110, 112, 114, 131–9, 164, 165–6
frappé 111
free thought 91
French Existentialism 91, 149
freshness 96–7, 113

## G

Gaggia, Giovanni Achille 122
gnosis 86, 91–2
God 26, 30
gratitude 70
greatness 38–9, 40
Greek coffee 110–11
Greek philosophy 29
ground coffee, smell of 160–2
gustation 165–6

## H

health benefits 81–2
Heidegger, Martin, *Dasein* 46–7
Hemingway, Ernest 84
history of coffee 15
Hui-neng 49
hulling 81

## I

Ibn Sina, *Canon of Medicine* 67–8
identity, definition of 52–3
Imamichi, Tomonobu 47
imperfection 77
individualism 46, 53–4, 55–6, 77, 99, 101
intimacy 93, 94–5
Islamic world 64

## J

Jesus 26
Jōdo Shinshū 146
Judaeo-Christian religion 29–31

## K

Kaldi 60, 61, 62
knowledge 86, 144

## L

lattes 132
Linji Yixuan 62
Lloyd's Coffee House 15
logos 86, 87, 91, 95

## M

medicinal properties 67–70
meditation 149, 162–3
mindfulness 128, 162–3

minimalism 99–100
moka pots 121
*mono no aware* 131
Moriondo, Angelo 121
Mormon Church 64
Muhammad, Prophet 59–60
myths, first cup of coffee 60–2, 64

# N
nature 75–6, 79, 82

# O
Okakura, Kakuzō 40, 41, 45, 46–7, 149
   *The Book of Tea* 21, 25–6, 28, 34, 37, 38, 47, 59, 93, 127
   'sympathetic communion of minds' 147
   Taoism 75
   tearooms 96, 98
   'utmost beatitude of the mundane' 135
   Zen Buddhism 84, 86
Oromo 109

# P
Paul, St 31
penny universities 91
people watching 91–2
phenomenology 46
phones 103–4
Picasso, Pablo 135–6
Plato 29, 30
pods 123
privacy 93–4

production of coffee 39, 80–1, 153, 154–7
productivity 15–16
Pure Land Buddhism 146

# Q
*quawah* 64

# R
al-Razi, Abu Bakr 67
religion: coffee's ambivalent relationship with 64, 67
   Teaism as a religion of aestheticism 75
   *see also* individual religions
Rhazes 67
roasters 143, 145
roasting beans 113, 114, 153
Rowling, J K 84

# S
samurai 103, 104
Sartre, Jean-Paul 54, 84
*satori* 145–7, 149
the self 51, 52–3
Shin Buddhism 146
*shokunin* 58, 118, 152
Silex coffee filters 121
smell 134, 160–2
speciality coffee 8, 10–11, 18

# T
Taoism 26, 43–71, 75, 84, 137
tasks 56–8

taste 132–5, 136, 160, 162–6, 167
tea 13–14, 15
   *The Book of Tea* 21, 25–6, 28, 34, 37, 38, 47, 59, 93, 127
   in Japan 32
   tea ceremonies 16, 25, 95
   tea masters 143
teahouses and tearooms 75, 76, 93, 94
   Okakura's description of 95, 96, 98
   samurai and 103
Teaism 25–6, 45, 59, 62, 75, 146
   link to Coffeeism 28, 29, 81
   'spirit of Eastern democracy' 128
temperature of coffee 80, 82, 164, 166
Turkish coffee 110, 111

## U
uniformity 99
Unsymmetrical, abodes of the 101–3

## V
Vacancy, abodes of 96, 99–103
vacuum pots 119, 121, 122

## W
*wabi-sabi* 77, 79, 84
weighing scales 158–9
wet method 81
wisdom 86, 144–5, 149
'women's petition against coffee' 65, 67
*wu wei* 58–9

## Y
Yirgacheffe 136

## Z
Zen Buddhism 26, 43–71, 84, 86, 137, 146, 147, 149, 152
Zhuangzi 47

# About the Authors

**Dr Julian Baggini** is a philosopher, writer and journalist who has written over twenty books on a wide variety of topics, which have sold over half a million copies in the UK alone. He has served as Academic Director of the Royal Institute of Philosophy and was also the co-founder and editor of *The Philosophers' Magazine.* Julian's books have seen great international success; his titles have sold in twenty-four territories (excluding the UK and North America) and have been translated into twenty-three languages. His bestselling titles include *How the World Thinks* and *The Pig That Wants to Be Eaten*, the latter of which was released in a new expanded edition by Granta in 2024. His most recent work, *How the World Eats*, was published in 2024.

**James Hoffmann** is the co-founder of Square Mile Coffee Roasters, a multi-award-winning coffee roasting company based in east London. He was the World Barista Champion 2007, having won the UK Barista competition in both 2006 and 2007. He has a YouTube channel with more than 2.4 million subscribers, where he makes videos about anything and everything to do with coffee, and an Instagram following of more than 770,000. He is the author of *The World Atlas of Coffee* (first edition 2014, second edition 2018, third edition 2025) and the *Sunday Times* bestseller *How to Make the Best Coffee at Home* (2022).

To the memory of Kakuzō Okakura, with deep gratitude.

First published in Great Britain in 2026 by Mitchell Beazley, an imprint of Octopus Publishing Group Ltd
Carmelite House
50 Victoria Embankment
London EC4Y 0DZ
www.octopusbooks.co.uk

An Hachette UK Company
www.hachette.co.uk

The authorized representative in the EEA is Hachette Ireland, 8 Castlecourt Centre, Dublin 15, D15 XTP3, Ireland
(email: info@hbgi.ie)

Copyright © Octopus Publishing Group Ltd 2026
Text copyright © Julian Baggini 2026
Text copyright © James Hoffmann 2026 (foreword and afterword)
Illustrations © Mariya Suzuki 2026

Distributed in the US by
Hachette Book Group
1290 Avenue of the Americas,
4th and 5th Floors
New York, NY 10104

Distributed in Canada by
Canadian Manda Group
664 Annette St., Toronto,
Ontario, Canada M6S 2C8

All rights reserved. No part of this work may be reproduced or utilized in any form or by any means, electronic or mechanical, including photocopying, recording or by any information storage and retrieval system, without the prior written permission of the publisher.

The Right of Julian Baggini (text) and James Hoffmann (foreword and afterword) to be identified as the Authors of this Work has been asserted in accordance with the Copyright, Designs and Patents Act 1988.

ISBN: 9781846016387
eISBN: 9781846016394

A CIP catalogue record for this book is available from the British Library.

Printed and bound in China.

10 9 8 7 6 5 4 3 2 1

Publishing Director Alison Starling
Senior Editor Alex Stetter
Art Director Juliette Norsworthy
Senior Production Manager Pete Hunt

Drawings by Mariya Suzuki (mariyasketch.com)
Illustration reference, p6: courtesy of Vaughan Allison, MIA MIA, Tokyo